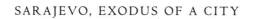

SARAJEVO, EXODUS OF A CITY

Sarajevo,

EXODUS OF A CITY

DZEVAD KARAHASAN

AFTERWORD BY
SLAVENKA DRAKULIĆ

TRANSLATED FROM THE SERBO-CROATIAN-BOSNIAN BY
SLOBODAN DRAKULIĆ

KODANSHA INTERNATIONAL
NEW YORK · TOKYO · LONDON

KODANSHA AMERICA, INC.
114 FIFTH AVENUE, NEW YORK, NEW YORK 10011, U.S.A.

KODANSHA INTERNATIONAL LTD.
17-14 OTOWA 1-CHOME, BUNKYO-KU, TOKYO 112, JAPAN

PUBLISHED IN 1994 BY KODANSHA AMERICA, INC.
THIS IS A KODANSHA GLOBE BOOK.

FIRST PUBLISHED IN SERBO-CROATIAN-BOSNIAN AS *Dnevnik selidbe*
BY DURIEUX PUBLISHERS, ZAGREB, 1993.
QUERIES ABOUT TRANSLATION RIGHTS SHOULD BE ADDRESSED TO
THE BUKOWSKI AGENCY, TORONTO.

PRINTED IN THE UNITED STATES OF AMERICA

94 95 96 97 98   6 5 4 3 2 1

LIBRARY OF CONGRESS CATALOGING-IN-PUBLICATION DATA
Karahasan. Dzevad.
   [Dnevnik selidbe. English]
   Sarajevo, exodus of a city / by Dzevad Karahasan : translated
from the Serbo-Croatian-Bosnian by Slobodan Drakulić.
       p.   cm. — (Kodansha globe)
   ISBN 1–56836–057–6
   1. Sarajevo (Bosnia and Herzegovina)—History—Siege, 1992–
—Personal narratives, Bosnian.   2. Karahasan, Dzevad.
I. Drakulić, Slobodan, 1947– . II. Title. III. Series.
DR1313.32.S27K3713   1994
949.702'4—dc20   94–5278

BOOK DESIGN BY KNUTE BREIDING

THE COVER WAS PRINTED BY PHOENIX COLOR CORPORATION,
HAGERSTOWN, MARYLAND

PRINTED AND BOUND BY QUEBECOR PRINTING,
FAIRFIELD, PENNSYLVANIA

Contents

Translator's Note and Acknowledgments

There is currently a debate about the name of the majority language of the former Yugoslavia involving claims that it is really two, three, or even more separate languages (Serbian, Croatian, Bosnian, etc.). For the purpose of identification on the title page of this book, the author has decided to use the term Serbo-Croatian-Bosnian, which is a new term in English. I have used Croatian, Serbian, and Montenegrin dictionaries in translating this book, since there are as yet no Bosnian dictionaries.

I wish to express gratitude to three people who helped improve my translation of Dzevad Karahasan's book, and to furnish notes that will make it more accessible to North American readers. Speaking about the translation, my thanks go to Denise Bukowski and Philip Turner, each of whom has a share in giving our readers a smoothly flowing English-language version of Dzevad Karahasan's work. As to the notes, I owe their accuracy to my Yugoslav émigré compatriot and friend, Mile Božicković, who quietly understands Yugoslav wars much better than many a pretentious expert. As to the remaining flaws and errors, they are mine alone.

SARAJEVO, EXODUS OF A CITY

Sarajevo, Portrait of an Internal City

SARAJEVO, THE CAPITAL OF BOSNIA AND HERZE-
govina, is the country's largest city. Founded by Isa bey
Ishakovic* in 1440, it is also a typical Bosnian city. Built
in the Milyatska River Valley, surrounded by mountains, Sarajevo is enclosed and isolated from the world, so to speak, cut
off from everything external and turned wholly toward itself.

At the flat bottom of the valley is a business center named
Charshiya, comparable to the downtowns of contemporary
European cities. On the inner hillsides that encompass the
valley are residential quarters called *mahalas*.†

In this way the city center is doubly enclosed from the
world: by the hills that encircle the city, and by the *mahalas*.
Because of the configuration of the terrain, as well as the
town plan, the *mahalas* function as armor, protecting the city
center from everything external, just as a snail or a clam is
protected by its armor.

Perhaps because this double enclosure forces Sarajevo to
"look into itself," soon after its foundation the city became a
metaphor for the world—a place where different faces of the
world gather at one point, in the way that scattered rays of
light gather in a prism.

Approximately a hundred years after its founding, the city
had gathered within itself people from all the monotheistic
religions and the cultures derived from them, with myriad
languages and ways of life. Sarajevo became a microcosm, a
center of the world that contained the whole world within
itself, as mystics would say.

---

* A *bey* was a minor local governor under the Ottoman Empire. Judging from his
full name, this one seems to have been a native Slav convert to Islam.
† Turkish, city district, or neighborhood in a wider sense.

That is why Sarajevo is an *internal* city in the meaning that mystics have ascribed to that word. Everything that is possible in the world existed in Sarajevo—distilled, reduced to its nucleus. Sarajevo was the center of the world, for the external is always and completely contained within the internal, and hence within the center as well. Sarajevo is like the fortune-teller's crystal ball that contains all events, all that any human being can experience, all the phenomena of the world. Like Borges's Aleph,* showing in itself all that ever was, that ever will be, and even all that could be, Sarajevo holds within itself all that constitutes the world to the west of India.

Perhaps that is so because Sarajevo is, like other Bosnian towns, so completely turned away from the external world, turned onto itself and into itself. That may have come about because in the world there is need for a city that could ideally contain the whole world within itself—like a crystal ball—and then again it may be for some other reason. I don't know why, but I know that it is so.

When it was founded, the city was settled by people from three monotheistic religions—Islam, Catholicism, and Eastern Orthodoxy—and the languages spoken in it were Turkish, Arabic, Persian, Bosnian, Croatian, Serbian, Magyar, German, and Italian. And then, some fifty years after Sarajevo was founded, the Spanish rulers Ferdinand and Isabella banished the Jews of Spain, some of whom took refuge in Sara-

---

* Borges himself defines the Aleph as "the only place on earth where all places are—seen from every angle, each standing clear, without any confusion or blending," adding that "the Aleph's diameter was probably little more than an inch, but all space was there, actual and undiminished." See Jorge Luis Borges, *The Aleph and Other Stories, 1933–1969* (New York: E. P. Dutton, 1970), pp. 23 and 26.

jevo. They brought to the city its fourth monotheistic religion and a new culture—constituted around that religion and around centuries of wandering—and they brought new languages, too.

Sarajevo became a new Babylon and a new Jerusalem—a city of new linguistic mingling and a city in which temples of all faiths of the Book can be seen in one glance.*

This mixture of languages, faiths, cultures, and peoples living together in such a small place produced a cultural system unique to Bosnia and Herzegovina, and especially to Sarajevo. It was clearly their own, original and distinctive. There were, of course, many regions and many cities in the ethnically and religiously mixed Turkish Empire where peoples, languages, and religions were entwined with each other. Yet there surely was no city—not even in that vast domain—where so many languages, religions, and cultures met and mixed with one another in such a small place.

Perhaps that can also explain why Bosnia had a special status within the empire, and why it was an autonomous *pashaluk*.† The singularity of the Bosnian cultural system demanded special political status. By the word *culture* I mean that which Claude Levi-Strauss defined as a way of life—all the acts and facts that shape everyday life.

The Bosnian cultural system—established in its purest possible form exactly in Sarajevo—could be quite precisely defined as "dramatic," as opposed to systems that could be

---

* In the Muslim tradition, the faiths of the Book are Judaism, Christianity, and Islam.

† Turkish, *pasha* = governor; *pashalic* = province.

described as "dialectical." The fundamental principles of the Bosnian cultural system are akin to the principles that constitute drama and can be understood in comparison to them.

Namely, the fundamental relationship between elements of the system is oppositional tension, which means that its elements are poised against one another, and mutually bound by that opposition, wherein they define each other. These elements enter the system—which is the totality of a higher order—without losing their primordial nature or relinquishing any of the properties they possess independently of the system to which they belong. Every element enters the system by acquiring new properties, instead of losing any of those it possessed from the beginning. Every one of these elements is itself a complex whole, composed of two parts, mutually connected by their oppositional relationship.

The fundamental property of this kind of cultural system is pluralism, which is what makes it directly contrary to monistic cultural systems, which can also be defined as dialectical. Monistic systems still prevail in the big cities of the West, with their mixtures of faiths, languages, and peoples, seemingly akin to the one in Sarajevo.

However, the fundamental relationship in a dramatic cultural system is the tension in which its elements confirm their primary nature. The fundamental relationship in a dialectical system is mutual devouring or—if this sounds better—the containment of the lower within the higher, or the weaker within the stronger.

Every member of a dramatic cultural system needs the Other as proof of his or her own identity, because one's own particularity is being proven and articulated in relationship to the particularities of the Other. But within a dialectical system an Other is only seemingly the Other, while it is actually the masked I, or the Other contained in myself. That is so because within a dialectical system, as well as in the dialectical way of thinking, opposite facts are actually One.

This is the fundamental difference between Sarajevo and contemporary Babylonian mixtures in Western cities. This difference requires an explanation, or at least a cursory description of the cultural systems constructed in these areas, even though it may be a bit technical.

The most pronounced trait of a dramatically constructed cultural system is an exciting interplay of dialogue and opposition between the open and the closed, the external and the internal. This interplay determines the internal organization of a city, as well as the structure of each of its parts, including its everyday life and even each of its elements, from dwelling to dining. The interplay can be observed at all levels, and it demonstrates yet another way in which Sarajevo is an internal city.

The interplay of that which is open and that which is closed, of the external and internal—which mutually comment upon, confront, and reflect each other—is made perfectly clear in the organization of the city. It has already been said that the business center of the city is literally situated at its most interior point, because it is doubly enclosed from the outside world: first of all by the hills that enclose the valley in which it was built; then again by the diverse city quarters, *mahalas*, built on the inner slopes of those hills.

The *mahalas* are like rays spread around a focal point. Hence, looking from the city center, on one side stands the Muslim *mahala* called Vratnik; on another side the Catholic *mahala* called Latinluk; on the third side the Eastern Orthodox *mahala* called Tashlihan; on the fourth side the Jewish *mahala* called Byelave. There are also some lesser *mahalas* (Bistrik, Meytash, Kovachi), each of them determined—just like the bigger ones—by one faith, one language, one system of customs.

The center of the city, which is also the geometrical center of the space outlined by the *mahalas*, is Charshiya, where people do not live because it is reserved for workshops, stores, and other forms of business. Charshiya, doubly enclosed from the outer world, is, in a technical sense, the very interior of the city—not just because of that double enclosure, but also because it is the geometrical center. Moreover, it is interior in the semantic sense, too, because an interior is always open—as mystics say—semantically open, because it holds within itself the potential of all that is possible in the exterior. Charshiya also contains all that exists around it, within those enclosures that separate and protect it from the outside world. At Charshiya, each culture that exists in the *mahalas* articulates and realizes its universal component. At Charshiya the universal human values—which of course exist in every culture—are being realized. Business goes on there, providing the economic foundation for existence in this world, and, simultaneously, human solidarity is being expressed at Charshiya, through communication and openness among people and toward one another.

For, at Charshiya, people from all the *mahalas* spread {9} around it, meet each other, communicate, cooperate, and live side by side. One beside the other are the shops of a Jew from Byelave, a Muslim from Vratnik, a Croat or an Italian from Latinluk, a Serb or a Greek from Tashlihan. And they all help each other, work with or against each other, support or cheat each other—or two of them versus a third—showing by that collaboration or by that conflict their elementary humanity, and thus realizing the universality of their cultures, actualizing that component that makes them universally human.

Charshiya removes the differences among Sarajevans that exist because of their being members of different cultures; it equalizes them in that which is common to them, what is universally human—in work, the need for material goods, love and envy, solidarity. At Charshiya, all of them are just people and Sarajevans, merchants and artisans, notwithstanding all the differences that exist among them. This is why Charshiya, the city center, is at once the most interior and the most open place.

Upon leaving Charshiya, all Sarajevans retreat from human universality into the particularity of their cultures. Namely, every *mahala* continues the enclosed lifestyle of the culture that statistically prevails in it. Hence, Byelave, for example, is distinctly a Jewish *mahala*, whose everyday life completely realizes all the particularities of Jewish cultures; life in Latinluk goes on in accordance with the particularities of Catholic cultures; in Vratnik in accord with Islamic cultures; and in Tashlihan according to the particularities of Eastern Orthodox cultures.

A Catholic in Latinluk is in the same measure and in the same way a Catholic as the one who lives in Rome, and a Muslim in Sarajevo with a house in Vratnik is a Muslim in the same way and in the same measure as the one who lives in Mecca. Perhaps even more so, because living in Sarajevo, all of these people have in their immediate neighborhood the Other, in whom they recognize their particularities and their own identity.

Latinluk borders on Bistrik, which means that Catholic and Muslim cultures touch upon each other. Because of that proximity and the continuous contact, Catholics and Muslims from those *mahalas* completely recognize their particularities, and completely develop consciousness of their own identities. Discovering the Other I discover myself, getting acquainted with the Other I recognize myself. Thus the *mahala*, which is at the outside, at the border or edge of the city, and which is technically open—because its back side opens toward the hill, nature, the outside world—reveals itself as semantically closed, after all, because its people live within one culture, acting out and realizing the particularities of that culture in their everyday lives.

This is the foundation of the interplay of opposition and mutual reflection, of openness and closedness, of external and internal that is the most prominent characteristic of Sarajevo. This is also the source of the tension between external and internal, upon which the very foundation of Sarajevo's existence is based.

Charshiya is technically closed and semantically open, while each *mahala* is technically open and semantically closed. Charshiya is universality; *mahala* is particularity and concreteness. Charshiya is enclosed from everything, and that is why it potentially contains all; *mahala* is open to everything, and that is why it has to enclose itself within its particularity. *Mahala* does that in order to survive, because in the external world only that which is defined and enclosed into some singular form can survive. Charshiya and *mahala*—universal and particular, open and enclosed, internal and external—always reflect each other as in a mirror, or like two parts of an inverse ratio.

This complex interplay of mutual opposition and reflection between the external and the internal—upon which the existence and functioning of Sarajevo are founded, and which is so clearly expressed by the relationship between Charshiya and the *mahala*—can be recognized in every segment of the city's existence and lifestyle. In the dwellings of the inhabitants, for example.

Sarajevans live in houses constructed on the hillside where their *mahala* is arranged. Every one of those houses has one side—the face, facade, the front—turned to the street, hence to the city, to Charshiya, to the center—while its other side faces the hill, nature, the outside world. At the front, the house is enclosed by a tall wooden fence, a veritable wall that renders the face of the house invisible from the outside; at the back, the side that is turned to the hill and nature, the house is open, only symbolically fenced in, and completely unconcealed.

At both ends of the house lie courtyards or gardens. At the front, between the wall and the face of the house, lies the front yard, which is entirely enclosed and fenced in at all sides. At the back, between the house and the hill, lies the back yard, which is closed at one side (by the house), and entirely open at the other (one could almost say that it naturally flows into the hill).

It is obvious in the structure of the house, and in the functional distribution of its gardens, that the same interplay is being repeated that we recognized in the very structure of the city—the living relationship between Charshiya and the mahalas. The face of the house is technically closed, as I said, because it is enclosed by a high wall over which human sight does not reach, enclosed from the street, from the city, and Charshiya, and from everything that stands in front of it. Yet, functionally and semantically, this face is open (it is, after all, turned to the center; it is the "internal side of the house") because one enters the house from this side, guests penetrate it from this side: on this side the house lives, and through this side its exchange with the world goes on.

The opposite side is technically open, because there the house is not fenced away from the world, but goes on instead, without interruption, to the garden, then to the hill, and then into "pure nature." Yet this is where the house is functionally and semantically closed, because at that side one only departs. At this side guests do not arrive, food is not brought in, one does not go off to work. At this side lies the exit, used only by the members of the household to go to the garden, so that there is no communication, or any exchange between the house and the outside world, that takes place at this side.

The situation is virtually identical for all of Sarajevo's courtyards and gardens. The front yard is technically perfectly closed—literally like a clamshell—because it is enclosed from all sides, either by the wall facing the street or by the house itself. One cannot enter it, and one cannot look in without the occupants' permission. Yet, functionally and semantically, this is the most open part of the house, where the household members take refuge from the world: through this opening guests, military and court summonses, food and policemen arrive; through this yard come all who wish to penetrate the house; and in fair weather people sit there with their guests.

The garden behind the house, the one open to the hill and nature, is technically entirely open (it is enclosed on one side only, by the house wall), but functionally and semantically it is entirely closed, because only household members enter it, and only directly from the house. That yard is closed to guests, closed to all outsiders, limited to the household members who lounge there, when they feel like doing so and when they have the leisure time.

The same goes for the house itself, because behind its walls the house is divided into open and closed, male and female quarters. Guests sit in male quarters, and strangers enter them as well; in the male quarters people talk about money and politics, about wars or the news of the world. Only household members may enter the female quarters, and even then only upon an invitation from within. In the female quarters people talk about food and love; in those quarters people make love, and children are born.

Seen like this, the living quarters of the inhabitants of Sarajevo are similar to the structural model of the city: a distilled city, a crystal bit of the mosaic in which the whole mosaic is reflected. In the quarters where the personal, intimate lives of Sarajevans go on, the same relationships are established, together with the interplay of open and closed, external and internal—relationships and interplay we recognized within the structure of the city; in the relationship between the city and its surroundings; in the relationship between Charshiya and the *mahalas*.

The same interplay can be observed in the gastronomic culture of the city dwellers. In Sarajevo, as in all other Bosnian cities, gastronomic culture is based on two culinary paradigms: one of them is extreme openness and the other extreme closedness. The open gastronomic paradigm consists of various kinds of meat, prepared over an open fire and meant to be eaten outside—in a restaurant, on a picnic, in a house that guests have entered. It can simply be a piece of meat roasted over the open fire, with the addition of some spices, and served in an open bowl, on a piece of clean paper, or on a piece of board. It can also be a more complex piece of culinary art, which nevertheless achieves a high degree of openness. Sarajevan kebab may be the most characteristic example of this culinary style. It is a dish that Sarajevans mostly eat outside, indisputable evidence of the openness and outwardness possible in a gastronomic culture.

Sarajevan kebab is prepared from ground meat and spices. Mixed together, they are kneaded into little cylinders that are phallic in shape, cooked on the open fire, and served on an open platter. Can there be more openness, more outwardness, more of a bared male principle?

Everything is exactly the opposite in the case of dishes of the closed gastronomic style. These dishes are prepared indoors, in a house free of guests, in the family circle; they are made from a mixture of vegetables, meat, and spices over a covered fire in tightly sealed pots.

Perhaps most illustrative of this gastronomic style—because it is most characteristic—is that group of dishes that go under the common name of *dolma* (filled food). *Dolma* are prepared with a filling, in a container that is filled. The filling is most often made of ground meat, rice, spices, and various kinds of chopped vegetables. The container can be peppers, opened by pulling out the stem; it can be hollowed potatoes or onions; it can be the leaves of cabbage, grape vine, kale, or some other leaf large enough and softened enough by cooking so that it can be wrapped around the little ball made of the filling.

If it is made from a pepper, hollowed potato, or a zucchini, the *dolma* has the shape of that which is filled; if it is wrapped in some kind of leaf, the *dolma*, as a rule, is shaped like the ball of the filling. That is how a piece of *dolma* looks, and when enough pieces are made, they are stacked in an amphora-shaped tureen that is then hermetically sealed with its own lid or with a piece of parchment tightly tied around the neck. The dish is then cooked on the low covered fire, long enough and slow enough to cook all the ingredients in their own juices. Every ingredient of a *dolma* must retain its original taste, and all of the ingredients together offer an entirely new, interminably complex taste that cannot be compared to anything or illustrated by such a comparison.

As can be seen from this description, a *dolma* is a dramatically constructed dish; it is characteristic of the dramatically constructed Bosnian culture; it resembles that culture and is completely at home in it. *Dolma* is a dish of the female principle—internal, closed. Because of that it is tolerant, accepting and embracing all flavors, so much so that it is considered a failure if a single one of its ingredients loses its original taste during the process of cooking.

Should the relationship between the two types of Bosnian cuisine be explicated? Should it be explained that this relationship repeats the interplay we have already recognized in the relationship between Charshiya and the *mahalas*, between front and back yards, between male and female quarters of the house? Should it be repeated that here, too, in its gastronomic culture, the totality of the city is reflected, in the same way that the whole mosaic of which it is a part would be reflected in a tiny crystal ball?

Should it be further explained that such a fine and complicated totality like Sarajevo—in which the entire country of Bosnia and Herzegovina is reflected as in a mirror—must be fragile? Should it be especially mentioned how natural it is that such a totality attracts and enchants prisoners of an epic culture just as the interior of a marble attracts and enchants savages? The fundamental difference should be stressed by all means, however: an enchanted savage admires the center of a marble, but he will never break the glass to get to it because the savage is reverent: he knows that the spell and the enchantment that make it all worthwhile would then disappear. But a prisoner of an epic culture—a culture that plays its music on a single string and is almost entirely contained in it—stares at Sarajevo and circles around it, while the city eludes him as the marble's eye escapes the savage. But then the epic man shatters Sarajevo, for he has lost his reverence and his ability to enjoy enchantment, because of the illusory nature of his epic cultivation.

In this book are a few stories about the shattering of Sarajevo, about the defilement of magic, and about the loss of the
ability to enjoy enchantment. These accounts are extremely
straightforward: their sole intention is to say how much every
simple fact hurts. Trust their author, who is otherwise a cool
and not particularly sentimental man, that the banal simple
facts of forced exodus hurt the most. Not only and not so
much the details of one's own actual exodus, like leaving
behind one's fountain pens, carpets, writing desk, and library;
what hurts much, much more is witnessing the veritable exodus of the city. It is this exodus that Sarajevo is going through
right now, passing from material to conceptual reality, from
its valley surrounded by hills to the sphere of memory, of
remembrance, of ideas.

Sarajevo, which was an internal city in the metaphorical
meaning ascribed to the word by the mystics, is becoming literally internal: stupidly literally. And literality hurts, believe
me. Sarajevo is ceasing to exist in the material (external)
world, because it is being destroyed and is moving into the
spirit (internal) world, and into the memory of those who
know it and love it.

Aspects of Marindvor

IMAGES OF MARINDVOR

MARINDVOR (MARIA'S COURT) IS A SQUARE apartment complex built in 1884, along four sides of a city block that used to be at the extreme periphery of Sarajevo, during both Austrian-Hungarian rule and the time of the First Yugoslavia.* Then it stood at the very edge of what was considered to be the city. Later it gave its name to a neighborhood. On the opposite side of the Milyatska River, less than a kilometer away from Marindvor, Sarajevo's Jewish graveyard stands on top of a hill. On its slopes are the villas that used to belong to wealthy Austrian officials, industrialists, and merchants.

The neighborhood where the country villas are located is called Kovachichi, which once was considered the border between human settlement and nature. Spreading from Marindvor on the right bank and Kovachichi on the left bank of the river, there used to be the pastures, wastelands, swamps, warehouses, and various other kinds of desolation that usually surround cities.

How peripheral Marindvor was in the minds of the Sarajevans of those times is indicated by an anecdote I heard from a lawyer friend of mine. In the first days of the Second Yugoslavia, right after the end of the Second World War, the authorities had accommodated nine members of shoemaker Abid's family on the ground floor of kebab-man Ismet's house. Five or six years after the war, in the fifties, Ismet's son

* The term "First Yugoslavia" is used for the Kingdom of the Serbs, Croats and Slovenes, later renamed Yugoslavia, in the period of 1918–1941.

got married and wanted to move to the ground floor of his parents' house. Ismet went to speak about that to Abid, suggesting to him that he request a new lodging from the state authorities.

"You are a proletarian," said Ismet. "They give you whatever you ask for, because they love proletarians."

My lawyer friend suggested that Ismet should require Abid's removal from his house, and that Abid should tell the court that he accepts it, because moving to another apartment would completely suit him. They did so, and when summoned to the court, Abid solemnly declared:

> Glorious court, I will move wherever I am told. I could even live at Marindvor, if that is in the interest of the people, and if my children will have a roof over their heads.

For Abid as well as for every other Sarajevan at the time, to live at Marindvor meant dwelling at the end of the world. That is why this anecdote touches me. I am really moved by Abid's readiness to sacrifice something for his involuntary landlord, and furthermore, to act in accordance with his sense of justice and moral obligations between people.

Through hurried construction of large residential suburbs, the Second Yugoslavia expanded the city limits far beyond Marindvor and Kovachichi in a matter of few years. This expansion was so huge that by the sixties, Marindvor had already become part of the center of the city.

When I moved to Marindvor, its central position had already been confirmed by the authorities themselves. They constructed buildings housing the Republic's government and Parliament at the very edge of that neighborhood. Because of this, people of my generation were perplexed by the fact that the mosque next to my building was called Magribiya. It was given that name in Turkish times because it stood at the extreme west of the city. Magribiya marked the western limit of the city (*magreb* means "west"). Now Marindvor is at the very heart of the city, while beyond Magribiya, much farther to the west, lie a series of temples, both older and newer structures.

In the last decade of the nineteenth century the owner of the Sarajevo brickyards, Mr. August Braun, started building the big residential block that he named after his wife, Marijin Dvor, or Maria's Court. The building was finished in phases spanning several years. It consisted of a large inner courtyard bordered by the four large wings of the building.

Those four wings delineated the four future streets of the new city block: one between Maria's Court and the Magribiya Mosque; another between Maria's Court and the Church of St. Joseph; one that ran toward the river; and one that went toward the hill in the back. Each wing of Maria's Court has two entrances. The southern and northern wings have three stories; the western and eastern have two. The inner courtyard of the block was embellished with flower gardens, plane trees, pathways and benches, from the very beginning.

The residents soon shortened the name of their building from Marijin Dvor, its full Bosnian name, to Marindvor, a contracted form of the name. This indicated their acceptance of the Austrian administration and its presence in Bosnia as a fact to which they were reconciled. This acceptance was supported by these facts: that the new authorities had constructed a lot of buildings and built them well; that they strove to make the new buildings familiar and acceptable to their local hosts; and that the Austrian authorities did not demand very much from their new subjects.

Soon, Sarajevans started thinking of the new buildings as their own, giving them new names, or altering their names to render them more familiar. In this way they expressed their acceptance of the new structures as their own.

A reliable symbol of that adoption is the construction of Haliddvor. Designed by the architect Josef Gramer, this residential and commercial building was completed in 1892 for the wealthy and well-respected Sarajevan Mustafa Hadzhibashchaushevich. Its construction definitively established the city block that remained the western border of the city for many years. By the beginning of the present war, it was considered to be in the city center proper.

Perhaps because of its central position, Marindvor is a neighborhood remarkably characteristic of Sarajevo. In one square kilometer there are: the Magribiya Mosque at the extreme western limit of the quarter, dominated by Turkish architecture; Marindvor and the Church of St. Joseph, which are typical Austro-Hungarian buildings; Haliddvor, an example of the Austro-Hungarian quest for a Bosnian architectural style; and the contemporary glass-and-steel constructions of Parliament and the government buildings.

That square kilometer contained a plain hamburger kiosk and the ornate Haliddvor. A single glance could include the modest Magribiya with its wooden pillars, the stone Church of St. Joseph, and the glass-and-steel government buildings or the Holiday Inn.

And then the war started, changing all that, a war that would impose a "military aesthetic" upon my city. In the generals' aesthetic view, Turkish, Austro-Hungarian and Yugoslav, Islamic, Catholic, and Communist buildings cannot remain side by side. Hence the suffering of the Marindvor neighborhood commenced, wasting and breaking up its constituent parts.

I have preserved several images of that Yugoslav People's Army orgy, in both my skin and my memory. In order to make my memories bearable, and in the hope that I might win a normal life and possess my own home once again—at least in the sphere of ideas—I have recorded some fragments about the exodus of Marindvor to the shadows of memory.

DESCRIPTIONS OF FEAR

I

Marindvor received its first furious blast of destruction toward the end of the fifth month of the year 1992. It was the night between the 27th and 28th, if I remember well. It started around nine in the evening and went on until four in the morning. They shot at us with their heaviest artillery shells. During the first few months of war, they usually opened fire at night, so that we were dazed all day long with sleepiness and fatigue.

It was dawn by the time that shooting subsided enough for us to leave our basements. Pale from fright, from the sleepless night, and from that distinct weariness a sleepless night brings about—which we knew so well by then—we convinced one another that we were "quite well, just a bit tired," and set off to check on Marindvor, to see if some of our building had survived.

At the eastern and southern wings were two huge holes some two meters across, ringed by the black halo of the burned facade. My own western wing bore only one such hole. The plane trees in the courtyard were hacked to pieces, one young linden tree was chopped down as if with an ax, and two huge craters gouged the lawn and the flower beds of our inner courtyard.

Things were even worse surrounding our building: the Magribiya Mosque had no roof or minaret; the Church of St. Joseph lost its roof; the Unis skyscraper was burned down; there were a few huge craters in the street.

At that moment and for the first time in some ten years of my living there, I took a careful look at my own apartment building. I saw, for the first time, that the molding under the roof was adorned with heads in baked clay; that between apartments the facade was decorated with half-pillars; that every story had its own distinct type of window. At that moment, for the first time, I could see that my apartment building was truly beautiful, and I felt that I loved it.

I also felt some similarity between us. I felt that my building's architecture neatly and discreetly escaped conformity with its diverse aesthetic forms. That fact made it so different from those contemporary residential cages, which can only be described as anonymous because they are so uniform. Therefore my beautiful building quite rightfully bears its own name—a proud and beautiful name, moreover.

I did not think about all this then. Neither was I capable of much thinking, nor was there any time for such luxuries, because the broken windowpanes had to be removed from their frames. Yet, now, as I write down some of the images that weigh upon my memory, I could swear that it was exactly then—when I noticed for the first time how beautiful my Marindvor is—that an overpowering and painful awareness swept through my mind: I was actually bidding farewell to my home. Up until then I had recognized my home, but now I could really see it; up until then I lived in it, while now I could truly feel it and love it. It means that I am parting from my home, which becomes another memory; we comprehend the full value of what we encounter only after it has moved from this world into the realm of memory.

Why do we see so much better with the eyes of memory than we do in reality, my God? Why do we feel more clearly with our memory than our senses? Why have I seen my house and fallen in love with it only as it started to crumble, when I am beginning to lose it?

Removing the broken glass from the window frames, so that some big piece would not fall to the sidewalk and accidentally kill an innocent passerby—as had already happened elsewhere in Sarajevo—I kept staring at my own hands, checking their reality from time to time. One crushing effect of this war on those who actually fare the best—that is, who have not been killed or wounded—is this loss of confidence in reality, or at least in one's own ability to experience reality.

They lose their world in the way I have lost my house as I looked at it, discovering how beautiful it was.

My next job was to secure additional protection for the basement windows. The citizens of Sarajevo met the attack on the city entirely unprepared because they did not believe that an army that has constantly been telling them it is theirs (the people's) will turn against them; although there were those who knew that after that army's attack on Croatia there would be an attack on Bosnia. But even these people met the terror without sandbags piled up in front of basement windows, because it was extremely dangerous to make visible war preparations. The Yugoslav People's Army occupied Bosnia with a massive force of soldiers and weaponry, and had arrested all those who publicly showed that they were aware of its intentions (like any other army of occupation, after all).

This is why there were no sandbags on the basement windows. The events of the previous night, which had left a huge missile crater in my street, convinced me that any opening above the ground is an open invitation for death to pay us a visit. The bricks we had in the basement were not enough, so I decided to take some ashlars* from the ruins of the Magribiya Mosque. How many missiles and shells must have hit it to raze it so thoroughly?

"Why are you taking them?" a neighbor asked. He probably thought that the ruins are of more value than myself, or he might be one of those optimists who believe that a rock left from a wrecked cultural monument has some cultural worth as well.

---

* Square, hewn stone used in building.

"May I take it?" I asked the imam of the Magribiya Mosque, who stood nearby.

"Of course," answered the imam. "If these stones end up saving someone's life, or just diminishing people's fear, they will be truly sacred. And that is what places of worship should do—they should liberate us from fear."

Unfortunately, there are ever fewer places of worship in Sarajevo, I thought as I lugged the ashlar. They are systematically destroying them, like everything else that gives identity and cultural value to the city. They are destroying them quickly and thoroughly, leaving less and less to defend us from fear.

2

Approximately ten days after this major shelling we gathered at the university, my students and I. The main entrance of the Academy of Theatrical Arts faces Mount Trebevich, which is held by the Serb gunners. It is has always been a popular picnic site for Sarajevans and its delights have been praised in many songs. It is now dangerous to the point of being entirely off-limits. So we made a hole in the courtyard wall and gained access to the basement entrance of the Academy.

The students were unusually delighted at this meeting. They were joyfully tidying up their college, planning course work, exulting, and prattling. We were cautiously and very wisely silent about those professors who had left at the outbreak of war. Students knew that I would not allow any reproaches on the professors' account, and I knew that students would not accept the arguments I would use to defend my colleagues. We were therefore silent on that topic.

Our happiness because of our return to work meant too much to us to spoil it with misunderstandings that could not be discussed because of their emotional nature. I am old enough to feel respect for fear. They are too young to get rid of their puritanism and ethical radicalism. Curiously enough, our silence was not intrusive, although it was the first time ever that my students and I had a "forbidden topic" between us.

We agreed that our first job should be to work on the graduation performances of the senior acting students. We could not organize normal classes for junior students, but we could help the senior ones to be graduated. Furthermore, our younger colleagues would still learn their basic skills by helping the older ones and acting in their graduation performances.

"Work as much and as well as you can, please," I used to say to my students. "Your work is the only thing that can liberate you from fear, for a moment at least, and help you preserve your human dignity, sensitivity, and reason. We are abandoned by other people, forsaken by good fortune. This world is leaving us behind, too, so we are abandoned even by the very material reality they have taught us to believe in.

"Only our work has not left us: what we learn and the trade we serve still remain as our defense. One of the fundamental functions of art is to defend people from indifference—and a human being is alive for as long as he or she is not indifferent.

"You are better than the gentlemen from the West, who are not helping us, although they can: you are better than them because you are alive and they are indifferent. You feel the pain, fear, hunger and thirst; you feel love and rage. And do you know

what those wretches are doing to feel something? It is all in vain,
they do not feel, they are indifferent.

"True, they are watching our misfortune like a badly directed
movie, but they are so intrigued by our misfortune and our lives
only because there is nothing to be seen in their own lives. They
wonder about us and observe us in order to see anything at all.
So I can assure you that you are better than them, albeit unfortunate; and therefore I implore you to work as best as you can,
because you can still find some refuge in your craft alone. Serve
your craft, and it will defend you from everything that assails
you, like a warm and dark womb."

I did not really have to give them this pathetic speech.
Actually, I did not have to tell them anything. They themselves demanded that we not lower the examination criteria
on account of war. They themselves made the timetable for
rehearsals and distributed the acting roles in the examination
performances. They themselves supplied the stage properties
and set up the stage. They worked better than they had ever
worked in peacetime. I would not have even dared to dream
of them working so hard under normal conditions.

In less than two months they staged four performances that
were played all over the city. Without electric lights; without a
stage separated from the auditorium; without the sets that can
be wheeled around; with literally nothing but actors desiring
to play their parts, the script, and the spectators desiring theater to be an important element of normal life.

During the first few rehearsals, students were bothered by
the shells that were falling nearby. They would lose their concentration; they kept pausing; they would give up for a
moment—and then go back again, searching for ways to

clearly articulate the story. And then they got so used to the shells that they simply stopped reacting to them; some even audaciously sought to find a way to include the shelling in their play as a special effect, or as an integral part of their personal performance.

It was similar with the audience. At first, they would react to shelling, but later, they gave themselves over to the performance, and with more pleasure than they ever did in peacetime. We even formulated a new definition of theater in Sarajevo: Theater is an actor and a spectator in an interactive relationship articulated by the script, and by the actors' performances—in the absence of shells or with shells that are far enough away not to kill the actor or the spectator.

Theater like this nurtures and shelters us from fear, like a warm mother's womb, or one of the still undestroyed places of worship.

3

During the month of August I worked on my new novel called *Shahriyar's Rings*. It would actually be more precise to say that I tried to work, striving to convince myself that I was working and that I could take refuge in my work from the reality that keeps slipping away from me, and from life that is becoming unbearable. I worked in the building across the street from mine, in a lawyer's office on the ground floor.

One day in mid-August my wife, Dragana, should have come to pick me up around five in the afternoon, so we could go have something to eat at our apartment. When she did not show up, I started back home and we met in the middle of our quite narrow street.

"Are we going to dine right away, or should I read you what I wrote first?" I asked her.

"Read it to me, we have time before dinner," she answered, and we moved toward the office. Before we stepped in, we heard a terribly strong detonation: a tank, and very nearby we concluded, since we were more than well trained in recognizing the artillery the Yugoslav People's Army had at its disposal.

I could not read, of course. After that first explosion, a whole series of detonations followed, rendering the human voice inaudible. (It is significant that people today are becoming ever more silenced about their work in the face of new intellectual and scientific achievements.) To tell the truth, I did not feel like reading anymore. Besides, the tenants from the building that housed the office soon gathered all around us. They used the ground floor as their sole shelter from the shells.

The bombing of the Maria's Court block lasted approximately three hours; so we went up to have our dinner around eight. We still did not feel like reading, and we could not anyway, because we did not have enough oil for both the oil lamp we had in our apartment and another one in the office. My wife entered her study, which is right beside the kitchen, holding my lighter and looking for something to eat—and returned right away with nothing edible in her hands.

"What do you think about Faulkner?" she asked me.

"I think that some things are worth reading at least once," I answered.

"Well, then you will have to give them to me again," said she, inviting me to her room.

Once I was in there, the reason for her question became apparent at first glance: a large piece of shrapnel had passed through the wooden window frame, shattered the glass of the book-case, and cut up the books lined up in double rows for lack of space. It had sliced in half a book of Faulkner's stories; a book of critical studies, *An Approach to Faulkner*, edited by my colleague Sonja Basic; *Hope Against Hope* by Nadezhda Mandelstam; and one marvelous old edition of *Green Heinrich* by Gottfried Keller*, which I bought in a secondhand bookstore in Zagreb and gave to her several years ago.

I must confess that the general's choice of books confused me. I understand about Mandelstam, all is clear in her case: that is a book about misfortune and love, so it is natural that Stalinist generals hate it, that shrapnel should cut it, that the army is against it. I have not asked myself any questions regarding Faulkner, to tell the truth, because I generally do not have too many questions concerning him. But I cannot figure out to this very day what wrong Keller had committed against the general and his shells.

Our sense of humor failed us, though, after we realized that, had we been at home during the bombing, my wife or both of us would have been in her study at the moment when the general directed his attention to our books. We would have been exactly in the path of his literary pursuits.

For a long time after that I could not even think about

---

* Gottfried Keller (1819–1890), Swiss poet and novelist. *Green Heinrich*, his first novel, was published in 1854, and in a revised edition in 1880.

work, yet I felt warm gratitude for my work and my books all {35} that time. Once again, and quite concretely, literature had saved me from reality and from those who wish to dictate that reality. It gave me refuge and, what is much more important, it saved the woman I love.

4

One day in October my colleague Zdenko Lesic, professor of Literary Theory at the Philosophical Faculty and the president of the Writers Guild of Sarajevo, came to visit me. This university professor and a renowned literary theorist came as a courier—to hand me an invitation for the meeting that would establish the PEN* center of Bosnia and Herzegovina.

"Why does it have to be you who delivers the invitations?" I asked, surprised.

"There is nobody else," answered my colleague Lesic. "I cannot leave it to someone else, because all kinds of things can happen to people moving around the city these days. I could not stand it if someone suffered death or injury because of something he did for me."

Later on he explained that founding the PEN center of Bosnia and Herzegovina is one of the most important actions of the Writers Guild. It was an action he personally cared about a lot. Precisely because of that and because of the dangers, he wanted personally to do all the work himself.

---

* The literary organization, with branches worldwide, dedicated to preserving authors' freedom to write and publish. In November 1993, benefits were held in many cities to raise funds for the establishment of the PEN center in Sarajevo.

For the founding convention, he wished to gather together all people he regarded as indispensable. He knew that I avoided all meetings and gatherings, even those concerning literature.

Even if there were no need to fear the misfortunes that might befall people who moved around the city, Lesic would distribute the invitations himself because he needed to be sure that everything would be done exactly as it should be. My colleague Lesic would have called me up even if somebody else delivered the invitations, because he knows my resistance to the institutional organization of writers and literature, and it was indeed important that literally all of us should be at that meeting. Not because of the sheer number of people in attendance, but because of the moral obligation of all of us to do all we could for the survival of culture in our city and country.

For as long as we keep thinking about literature, greeting each other as our upbringing requires, and using cutlery while dining; for as long as we keep wanting to write or paint something, or endeavoring to articulate our situation and our feelings by means of theater; for as long as we defend our city and the tolerance that reigns in it; for as long as we retain our right to a common life among different nations, religions, and convictions, we still have a chance to survive as cultural beings. That is why it was so important for all of us to be there, to attend the founding convention of the PEN center of Bosnia and Herzegovina.

I had no objections to the reasoning of my colleague Lesic. So, two days later, on a marvelous October morning full of light and colors—of a kind that rarely comes to Sarajevo—I set off for the Holiday Inn. There are no more than five hundred meters between my home and the hotel, but that route could not be used because of the snipers. So I departed by way of the former military hospital, which is a roundabout course, five times longer than the normal one, but somewhat safer—or at least providing an illusion of safety, which was just about the same thing in our situation.

When I was about to leave home we could hear detonations, but I kept persuading myself they were quite far away and that I could go on. As I walked down the street that bears the name of the great poet Silvije Strahimir Kranjcevic—the same street where the Writers Guild is housed and, most important, a street that was relatively well protected from snipers—the detonations grew ever stronger, meaning that the source of the explosions was getting nearer. Neither this nor any other street is really protected from shelling, because—as it would be stated in military terminology—the artillery fire covers every point of our city: every kitchen and bedroom, every hospital bed and school bench.

I kept going on nevertheless, convinced by the reasoning of my colleague Lesic and feeling obliged to do as much as I could for the founding and functioning of the PEN center in Bosnia and Herzegovina. I admit that I could not see how a PEN center could secure better literature in the world, or how it could achieve an even far more important thing: namely, to ensure that existing literature would be better read. Yet I know that in the situation we have been brought to in Sarajevo, the founding of such a center is more important than the writing of good literature. It is even more important than the reading of good literature, because such a center can help save our bare lives and because it is a form of culture, and we can survive only through the cultural forms of existence.

At the PEN center, all of us will gather: Jews and Muslims, Serbs and Croats, Turks and Albanians—all who live here, with all our differences—will get together and talk, engaged in common work by which we help defend our common city and our right to live together. I would say that something more important than writing good literature is being accomplished in that work, something more important than any single individual act. More important in this—and only in this—moment.

So I went persistently on, contrary to reason and in spite of my own fear, intensified by the empty street. It is interesting how an empty street intensifies fear in times like these. In times of peace I used to love the empty streets. Because of that love I took my walks mainly at night, when the streets are conveniently empty, while now, a nighttime walk would be too terrifying.

Between Marindvor and the railway station, I asked some soldiers how I could reach the hotel. They gave me directions, but ended with advice to give up my visit there, because of the heavy shooting.

"I must go," I replied, thanking them for directions. And then I tried to make a little joke: "I am going to found a PEN center, and that is very important."

"If it is destined to be founded, it will be founded just as well without you," replied their commander. "So, just go ahead nicely to the shelter."

He motioned toward a basement door, sending one of his soldiers to summon to the shelter all the passersby he could find, especially those who are founding something.

"I must go anyway," said I, driven by the feeling of a debt owed to Lesic and my city and my pride, which would not let me be talked out of my decision so easily.

"Listen, man, we have the means to stop you, and we will use them if you don't obey me," said the commander, without any visible nervousness.

"But it will be just me who gets hurt if something happens," I protested.

"That would not bother me," answered the commander. "And I would not stop you for that reason. But I am the one who has to pull you out and bury you if something should happen to you—and I don't feel like doing that at all."

I had nothing to say against such strenuous arguments; so I followed him to the basement, which was proudly called "the shelter." There were many people down there already, who gathered from the street when the attack started. They were there long enough to form little groups, immersed in discussion. So I was left alone with my own questions.

The detonations had become so strong and close that it occurred to me several times that it may indeed be better for the PEN center of Bosnia and Herzegovina to be founded without me. I also thought, more than once and with gratitude, of the calm commander who did not want to bury me. Was there any sense in continuing my journey, after the attack waned a bit? Would the founding convention be held nonetheless? How and where had my colleagues, who were arriving from more distant parts of the city, found shelter?

Finally, the most essential and painful question remained, preventing me from joining any of the groups of talking people: What happened to my wife? She should have been at the radio station at that time, speaking about possible activities to help disabled children, or children who had no one left to take care of them, who were being sheltered by humanitarian organizations.

After the shelling abated a little, I went back home, attempting to convince myself that I would find Dragana at home. My colleagues continued on their way from the shelters to the hotel and met after all, founding the PEN center of Bosnia and Herzegovina, and giving me a lesson in stubbornness as well as renewed confidence that goodness still prevails.

My colleague and friend Tvrtko Kulenovic, President of the PEN center of Bosnia and Herzegovina, told me at length later on about the course of the founding convention. He told me also about the shelter where he himself found refuge that day. After that he amicably consoled me about my absence from the convention, assuring me that everything went on without me just as it would have gone on with me. The same, through and through. And the only thing that matters is that the work goes on, and that we preserve at least some measure of cultural life.

There, that was my role in founding the PEN center of Bosnia and Herzegovina.

THE DISTRIBUTION OF SHAME

I

In the beginning of November 1992, on a beautiful and relatively peaceful morning, I took off looking for water. In front of the door to a ground-floor apartment I found a neighbor in tears, sitting on one of the chairs where we used to sit when the city was being "moderately shelled." I asked her why she was crying and if I could help, but she just waved her hand at me and kept on crying. Some ten minutes later she responded to my repeated questioning, saying that she was crying because her children were with her, in Sarajevo.

Another neighbor, Radmila, had left Sarajevo that morning, together with her two little girls. She went to France with the United Nations Protection Force (UNPROFOR), to have a surgical operation performed on her daughter Nana, who was wounded by shrapnel that hit her in the face in our courtyard, during the mid-July shelling. Between July and November Nana's eyesight kept weakening, and the doctors in the Sarajevo hospitals did not dare perform the operation she needed.

This is why Mrs. Maria cried: She cried because her own children were not wounded, and so they had to stay with her in Sarajevo. When I finally understood her, I realized that my city ceased to be real at that moment, because it turned our familiar reality around the way a mirror reverses an image: all the joy, pleasure, and beauty of real life turned into pain today.

I thought about that until late afternoon, struggling with

witticisms about mirrors and unreality, to protect myself from the bitterness that kept sneaking in during that morning conversation. By evening, however, my thoughts were cast aside by a question, spoken out loud clearly with my own tongue: God, why do you let a mother mourn because her children are with her?

2

About one month later, in December of 1992, I was helping my wife, who is the chair of the humanitarian organization Our Children, to bring in and sort out the used clothes collected from the citizens of Sarajevo. We were in the middle of our work when a man walked in looking for something warm for his four-year-old son.

"If there is something, and"—he stressed—"if it is not from UNICEF."

I knew that he insisted on this because of the terrible humiliation that UNICEF subjected Sarajevans to not so long ago. They proclaimed a Children's Week in the beginning of November 1993, and then drove truckloads of clothes into Sarajevo that were made in Serbian factories and bought in Belgrade.

Such a move on the part of UNICEF seemed natural enough to me, because it is entirely normal that a UN organization should be the first to officially and publicly violate its own embargo on trade with the aggressor. My fellow citizens, however, who persistently wished to believe in the West, the United Nations, and so on, were deeply hurt by the incident.

They were hurt so much that they refused to take anything at all, if it came from UNICEF. My wife had already told me about that during the glorious UN Children's Week. That is why I was not surprised by the attitude of my fellow citizen who preferred to wrap his son in a blanket rather than dress him up in a gift from the humanitarian organization UNICEF.

Although I shared his feelings, I tried talking to him, to convince him to change his mind. I told him that it is wrong to think like that about all of UNICEF, because that incident involved one anonymous official waiting for his retirement to come. I said that this official did not mean to humiliate us, because he is so indifferent about everything that he has not felt even his own humiliations for who knows how long by now—not to mention wanting to humiliate us. I told him that he should not worry about sleepy UN officials, but about his child, and that his child is the only one that matters.

"My child has all he needs, thank God," answered my fellow citizen after the torrent of words I poured out trying to convince him. My eloquence actually increased as my own agreement with what I was saying decreased.

"What does he have?" I asked, angry because of my failure to convince him.

"He has an opportunity to die," he answered.

I never even tried responding to such an argument. I am aware that that was an expression of indifference as well. I know that my fellow citizen and I are as indifferent as those whom we criticize for their indifference, but I also know that our indifference is of an entirely different kind. I also know that the answer that we had discovered does not depend on the UN, the West, and indifferent officials, thank God. To this very day I feel deeply grateful to my fellow citizen, yet I never even learned his name.

3

On that same day I received a letter from my friend Albert Goldstein. He is a Sarajevan who has been living in Zagreb. I do not know how the letter arrived in Sarajevo, since postal service has been unreliable for some time. I just know that a friend from the hospital brought it to me, and that it was unusually long—two large pages written in tiny, almost illegible handwriting.

At that time of the year in Sarajevo, night falls in the early afternoon. That friendly letter had thus put in front of us a very difficult choice: We could not read it while there was daylight, because daytime had to be used to fetch drinking water and something to eat, and we could not read it at night, because Goldstein's handwriting was too minute to be read by an oil lamp. So I carried the unread letter around in my pocket for a few days, unable to choose between the wish to read some friendly words and the need to save oil.

The Yugoslav People's Army made my decision for me, as in so many other matters. They shelled Maria's Court with tanks and heavy artillery fire one night, badly wounding one neighbor. The next day we were tired, sad, hopeless; so my wife remembered the letter that proved that we are not alone in the world. (The proof of one's existence is not in your own thinking, as a certain French gentleman suggested with his phrase, "I think, therefore I am." Instead, the proof that I indeed exist is given by somebody else thinking about me.)

I lit two more oil lamps, put the letter on the table, surrounded it with all three oil lamps and started deciphering Goldstein's handwriting. For three evenings in a row we went on prodigiously burning oil, trying to read a letter full of friendly concern and sympathetic understanding of our problems.

That extravagance left us without oil, but it renewed our hope, our feeling that we really exist, our wish to talk to the people dear to us once again. In our personal calendar, the only one that makes sense during war, we have named those three nights spent over the illegible letter of a friend the "orgy of consolation." If I see Goldstein once again, I will not check whether he remembers what he wrote in that letter: I have not managed to decipher it all in spite of our great expenditure, and I would forgive him if he is unable to remember. Actually it does not matter; what matters is having a letter from a friend under our circumstances.

4

In the middle of January 1993 I received a visit from an American journalist accompanied by his translator, who happened to be my friend Aida Cerkez. Just as we sat down, a tank shell hit the roof of my building, so we dashed down to the basement. Just before the shell hit, the journalist had asked me, "How do Sarajevans feel now?" Once in the basement, I replied, "Like this."

He laughed sourly at my wisecrack and repeated his wish to hear about how Sarajevans feel now, when they have finally realized that the world will do literally nothing for the salvation of their city. Not knowing how to answer such a question, and unprepared to speak about my own feelings to a man I did not know and in front of all my neighbors, I went on theorizing about the productiveness of defeat. I gave examples of the Germans and the Japanese, who were the only ones to benefit from the aftermath of World War II, which they had lost. I also said that to be liberated from one's own delusions is a great benefit.

I spoke to the journalist, convincing myself that my students and I, if we survive, could only benefit from this horror, because art is truly constructed from the worst human defeats. The practical American, unprepared for my theorizing and my skeptical search for nuances, asked why we Sarajevans didn't accept the partition of Bosnia and the city, if that could be the way to peace.

I replied that I wholeheartedly agreed, if he could only propose the way to divide Bosnia and Sarajevo. As my neighbors were taking shelter in the basement (shells literally pouring down around the building), I could concretely demonstrate to the American a sample of the ethnic structure of Bosnia and Sarajevo within our building. Pointing my fellow tenants out, one by one, I showed that only one out of ten married couples occupying the ten apartments in the building is of the same ethnicity. I myself noticed that fact only then.

"How could you possibly divide that?" I asked. If Sarajevo were to be divided, I could not have a bath because the tub would remain in the Serb province of my wife; my Serb wife could not wash her face, though, because the washbasin would remain in my province. The same goes for nine out of ten apartments in our building. I am afraid that that could be complicated even for such an able divider as Mr. Cyrus Vance.

With extreme astuteness the American concluded that Sarajevans are being shot at because both those who are doing the shooting, and those who could but will not stop them, cannot divide that which is indivisible.

"That is correct," I agreed, elated by my guest's sense of logic. What is happening to us could be compared to a mathematics professor who is enraged by a pupil who persistently calculates that one multiplied by one is one. In the end, the furious professor kills his pupil, although the pupil could not possibly get a different result, in spite of the fact that he simply worked on a task given him by the professor himself.

"And you would otherwise agree to the division?" double-checked the American.

Aida and I agreed to the division in the name of our neighbors, if we would be allowed to keep our apartments, marriages, and lives. "Karadzic is a physician, by the way, not a notary, so it is not his job to divorce us," remarked my spouse.

"I don't understand how you can take all this," the American journalist said in the end. Aida and I looked at each other sadly and with a strong feeling of guilt. "You suffer, and you are completely innocent," said the journalist again, after neither of us answered.

"They don't understand anything," said Aida, after a prolonged pause.

"It is because they don't suffer," said I. "Suffering is an important form of cognition: it provides a kind of knowledge that can be acquired only that way, but we love to leave such knowledge to others."

"I would not cede mine to anybody," said beautiful Aida. "Believe me that I would not change places with any of them."

ON HUMAN ENVY

Many aspects of the siege of Sarajevo are reminiscent of medieval wars and the sieges that occurred in that time. The similarity lies not only in the complete encirclement of the city, coupled with "scorched earth" tactics, but also in the use of "auxiliary instruments" of warfare.

By "auxiliary instruments" of war I do not mean the weapons themselves, of course, which are quite modern in this case, and far more deadly than their medieval counterparts. I am talking about the way in which the weaponry is being used, and the ways in which this war has been waged; about devices that are not weapons pure and simple, but that kill human beings nonetheless.

One of the characteristic indirect instruments of warfare is the killing of the city and its inhabitants by hunger, thirst, and the withdrawal of the basic prerequisites of human existence. From the very beginning of the siege, the Yugoslav People's Army did not allow water and electricity, food and medicine, fuel, and articles for the maintenance of basic hygiene to reach Sarajevo.

As far as I know, that method of warfare was applied for

the first time and with terrifying efficiency during the first crusade undertaken on European soil—the war of the French king and Count Simon de Montfort against the Cathars,* Albigensians, or whatever they used to be called in Languedoc. Monsieur Simon de Montfort and his successors used to besiege cities like this, completely encircling them and driving them to a quiet death by denying them food and water. Montsegur, for example, was besieged for ten months and completely destroyed in March of 1244.

Bosnia was a Cathar land in those days as well, infected with the plague of Cathar heresy no less than Languedoc, and perhaps even more completely and profoundly. The Bosnian Cathars fared well then, however, much better than their brothers in France: they were not invaded by French crusaders at least (although they were attacked by Hungarian crusaders), and they were not utterly exterminated or starved to death.

Bosnians were always a type of Cathar, for they were—or wanted to be—"the third option" (*tertium datur*, as the Bosnians keep saying, contrary to the highest authorities). Is it possible that the time has arrived for Bosnians to suffer now what they had escaped before, aided by their Good God, at the time of Monsieur Simon de Montfort? They are being starved and their cities are being destroyed with an ardor that has not been seen since the time of Monsieur de Montfort—

---

* The Cathars, who believed in purging the body of sin through fasting (from which comes the English word *catharsis*) were related to the Albigensians, a heretical sect that originated in the Middle East but spread throughout Europe, in diverse forms. Its early European homelands were today's Bulgaria, Macedonia, Serbia, and Bosnia and Herzegovina, where some rulers were Bogomils (the Slavic name of the sect).

and all that with the wholehearted assistance of de Montfort's successors, who govern France today.

Is it possible that the passionate soul of Monsieur de Montfort has not calmed down in all this time, but is still restless, inhabiting the body and dressed in the uniform of a Yugoslav People's Army general, pulverizing Cathar lands, and eradicating Cathar seed among the people? He assaults all people except those verified as his own, for there could be some Cathar seed in everyone. One wonders with anxiety whether that seed could be tenacious enough to prevent the passionate de Montfort's soul from ever calming down and resting in peace.

He kills those Serbs who are not certified as his own. He kills them in the name of Serbdom, as he used to kill Christians in the name of Christianity in days of old.

"Kill them all, and the Lord will choose the true believers when they come to him," answered Pope Innocent II to a question about what the Crusaders should do in view of the presence of some true believers in the besieged Montsegur. The same thing goes on today, only the names are different. Why, and until when, for God's sake?

Is it possible that he will exterminate us all, just because we are the descendants of the Bosnian Cathars, whom he had no time to annihilate in the Middle Ages, when he destroyed the French Cathars with fire and hunger? Is it possible that it was written in the secret book of history—in those bygone times—that Bosnia must be destroyed, so the work initiated then is being completed now?

I keep scrutinizing such questions every time I go to fetch

some water from the basement of the building that used to house the Assembly of the Republic of Bosnia and Herzegovina. It is a sad ruin now. I don't dwell upon such questions because a trip to the basement would inspire me to ponder historical inevitability and the bizarre propensity of history to restore some of its past figures—like Monsieur de Montfort, for example. I scrutinize them because the way to that basement—one of three places where one can occasionally find some water—is very dangerous: so, by theorizing about the logic of history, I struggle to dispel my fear. And when I think like that, the damn fear intensifies, because the analogy between Bosnia now and Languedoc then removes every hope. Nonetheless, I keep theorizing on, I deduce analogies, I search through history, looking for models for Bosnia's fate.

Around the middle of January 1993, on an icy day with a temperature of one degree Fahrenheit, I remembered a case that may have been the first example of using hunger and thirst for military purposes, and the first example of a concentration camp in history. I remembered the inglorious fate of the Athenian men who had set off to Sicily, on a campaign against Magna Graecia, in order to turn the course of the Peloponnesian War in their favor. They were captured, locked up in an abandoned quarry, and kept there by their Greek brothers, with enough food and water to let them survive, though without assuaging their hunger or quenching their thirst.

I stood in line for water, looking around for someone I could talk to about this. It would have been good to talk for a while. My interlocutor and I could comfort each other by repeating long enough how lucky it is that Sarajevo is in a temperate climate zone, for example. What would happen and how would it be if we were living in the torrid Sicilian climate, in an abandoned quarry, with as little food and water as we have now?

The ruins left of our city still protect us from the cold and the burning sun. They protect us just enough to let us endure all this somehow, I smugly thought. Actually, I struggled to think smugly and to convince myself that such thoughts can diminish the cold, fear, and the urge to be somewhere else, even though that other place may not be my proper place.

It seemed to me that the serious gentleman two places ahead of me in the water line-up might be an interesting conversationalist, a man capable of encouraging-sounding chatter. He looked like a retired high school teacher, and such people are always ready for a conversation that seems to be sagacious; they are inevitably eager to talk about a better future and bright prospects.

It would be good if that man turned out to be a retired high school teacher, because at that moment I definitely needed a professional optimist. I would give a kingdom for a man who would speak up optimistically, even if both of us knew that he is lying. I decided to address that man, but I would not do that before thinking of a way to end the conversation if it turned out that I had made a mistake. My prospective interlocutor might not be a professional optimist, but one of those people, increasingly numerous in Sarajevo, who search for people to talk to in order to tell them about all the terrible things that still lie ahead of us.

I noticed that such people had been multiplying since last

summer, and ever since then I have been looking for ways to protect myself from them, because I have no reason at all to be the victim of their subterfuge, which I call a martyr's tactic. They seize on someone, dump upon him all that lies in their hearts, explain to him that there is no hope for anything, and leave—relieved at least by as much as talking about trouble can reduce it. Their listener remains burdened with their trouble on top of his own, however.

So they operate like professional martyrs, the impossible sort of people who blackmail all around them with their sensitivity, incessant suffering, and goodness, regularly throwing at least some of their problems upon the people around them. I had to think of a way to protect myself from this man ahead of me, if he also turned out to be a recent convert to martyrdom. That kind of person keeps multiplying as life in Sarajevo becomes less endurable.

Before I had figured out anything intelligent to say, the people in the line-up behind me became disturbed, as if something unusual was happening. My target interlocutor turned around and moved toward the end of the line. Others followed his example, so I also left my canisters and moved to the back, where a little group was gathering.

The group stood around a not very old man who had arrived shortly after me. After some ten minutes of waiting he had stepped out of the line, leaned against the basement wall, and motioned with his hand to all who came after him to freely go ahead. It turned out that the man who had motioned to all the others to go ahead of him while he sat with his back against the wall—as if resting—had died.

We hadn't had enough time to pull ourselves together, not quite believing that the man had died, when the ambulance people appeared among us. It is fantastic how quickly ambulances arrive where they are needed since the war started. These battered vehicles, riddled with bullet-holes and reduced to half their prewar number, appear suddenly as if they knew in advance where they were needed. If they were half this fast in peacetime, Sarajevo would have been the city with the best ambulance service in the world.

The people in white pushed their way among us, looked at the man, touched him a little, and sized him up. Then they waved their hands, giving up. They told us that he had no need for them, but for others they would send as soon as they could. Then they left, leaving us behind with the man who quietly let everybody step ahead of him.

We kept standing around our dead man, not even thinking about dispersing. Our canisters kept our places in the lineup for us, so only those whose turn came to fill them up left our group. The rest of us stood there in silence, watching the dead man, avoiding looking at one another.

Confused by what I felt, I looked at the people around me, convincing myself that they felt the same: in the looks of all of them could be seen, as clearly as if it had been written down in letters: envy. I felt the same, and that is why I kept looking at the people around me, to check it out. We envied that quiet man who so peacefully gave passage to anyone who wanted it, to go ahead and leave him behind.

Why did we envy him? Because he died so quietly and peacefully—so to speak, naturally—in this city at a time when such a death has become a rare privilege? Because of the courage we still do not possess to move over to the other side and escape all the problems and troubles that torment us? Because he did not wish to leave Sarajevo, the place allotted to him by destiny, while the rest of us wished to leave, because we could not take it anymore—regardless of how well we knew that people can feel right only in their own proper place, and that our own place was right there, where it was so unbearable?

He is in his own place now, and he does not need to leave. He does not envy those who are elsewhere, regardless of their condition. Perhaps we envied him for that. I don't know, but I do know that we envied him, and that is the whole truth.

Understanding War

AN ARGUMENT WITH A FRENCHMAN

IN BESIEGED SARAJEVO, AT THE BEGINNING OF DECEM-
ber 1992, I talked to a well-intentioned and sagacious man
from France. Our conversation lasted for more than four
hours, and it ended pretty ingloriously, because the good man
from France ended up being hurt, while I felt weighed down
by guilt. I have analyzed our discussion, reconstructing it several times in my memory, sincerely striving to understand it. I
examined the drama that determined our emotional and logical affinities and persuasions, and also through them the
outcome of our conversation—with which neither I nor the
noble Frenchman as satisfied.

Now I am trying once again to understand our discussion,
to analyze its dynamics, to decipher the reasons why our
exchange ended as it did. I am trying to draw my reader into
my attempt to understand, because I hope that your disinter-
ested view will help me to comprehend, or at least to articulate, what consistently keeps eluding me.

What is the issue at stake here? How did our conversation
proceed?

My guest asked me how I managed to live without running
water, and I replied that there sometimes is running water,
and that rain falls too, so one can collect the rainwater from
the drainpipes. And then I tried to explain that it is more
important to save Sarajevo and the possibility of the four
religions and four peoples living there together, than to be
concerned with having enough water.

Without listening to my theorizing about the advantages of cultural pluralism and the beauties of life in such an atmosphere, my dear guest from France asked what I eat under the present conditions in the city, where literally even birds don't enter the town. I answered that there is no great hunger in the city yet, that I have lost only five kilograms, and that it is most important now to prevent the non-Serb ethnic groups from answering with their own brands of chauvinism the Serb chauvinism that threatens everybody in the city, including those Serbs who have not succumbed to the chauvinism of the political leaders. And I went on theorizing about Sarajevo being the second Jerusalem, because only in Sarajevo and in Jerusalem do the temples of all four monotheistic religions exist and function in such a restricted space.*

I could not finish, because the Frenchman was interested in how I endure the five-degree Fahrenheit cold, in an apartment with no glass in the window frames. Answering him, I sincerely struggled to convince him that it can be endured: so I displayed my arms and legs that bore no traces of frostbite; I strutted around waving my hands in front of him; I hopped about and did all manner of things to show him that cold is not such a problem. But it is a problem, I kept saying, if only one Jerusalem remains in the world, because the whole world must be shown the embrace of all four faiths gathered in more than one place in order to be convinced that it is possible, and in order for us to really experience this reality.

---

* The author is obviously referring to Islam, Judaism, Roman Catholicism, and Eastern Orthodoxy. To some North American readers, it may seem strange to distinguish in this way between the latter two faiths, but it is clearly not unusual among natives of the former Yugoslavia.

Our conversation went on like that for about four hours: my guest kept inquiring considerately about the mundane problems of my everyday life, while I labored to show him that I am not all that bad off, because there are many people out there who have it much worse. Moreover, I exerted myself to draw the Frenchman's attention to what I feel to be the main cause of all my petty problems, as well as the source of the major problems of so many other people.

I kept saying that in some parts of the city people carry their feces around wrapped in paper, to throw them away at some hidden place, because there is no water with which to flush their toilets. So I was quite privileged, thank God, that I never once had to give up brushing my teeth for lack of water. Was it not clear how well off I was?

Is it clear to you, that all the problems—my little ones and other people's big ones—come from the fear of cultural pluralism that has decisively determined certain politics, and turned weapons against those who wanted to live together and rejoice in their differences? However, to all my attempts to convince him that I am better off than I deserve, the Frenchman responded by repeating that I must be feeling terrible.

After four hours of freezing together, we parted ways—the Frenchman hurt by my not suffering as much as he thought I should suffer, and me weighed down by guilt for having hurt a noble and well-intentioned guest who traveled such a long way to feel sorry for me and to do a good deed for me.

Why did our talk go that way? Why did we talk to each other for so long without communicating, and in truth without ever entering into a dialogue? How could it ever happen that the two of us would invest such huge and sincere effort in talking to each other, and yet not succeed in understanding each other at all?

Quite the contrary, we parted ways divided by a deep mutual misunderstanding, deeper and more hopeless than the one that stood between us in the beginning, when we first met. Before we started talking there was hope at least, and an abundance of good intentions. After we said to each other what we did, there was just the feeling of being hurt on his part, and the feeling of being guilty on mine.

When my Frenchman entered my home I was moved, grateful and prepared to do anything to show him how much this visit from the faraway world meant to me. When he entered my home, my Frenchman was overwrought by the tribulation of my city, filled with good intentions and determined to do something noble for me personally as well as for all of us. Our encounter was therefore elevated and graced by beautiful, noble feelings. Our attempt to communicate was similarly founded on an entirely sincere effort to understand each other, and to agree.

Why was our parting so bitter, then? Am I indeed such an ungrateful scoundrel, because I wasn't suffering as much as my guest had expected and had decided for me to suffer? Was my guest truly so shocked by my suffering that his emotions obstructed his view of the causes behind that and other, much greater suffering? Was my suffering truly enormous, and I have become so numb that I cannot see its dimensions and feel its depths anymore?

Such questions bothered me the whole night long, a night

filled with sadness and guilt, and in the days following it, while standing in the bread line-up, creeping between sniper bullets to get some water, or covering my ears with my hands in the basement to mute the sound of shells exploding outside. Those same questions I asked myself I have also asked my wife, a Serb whose mother was killed by the Serbs for sheltering two Muslim families in her apartment. She knew no more than I.

And then one time while working in the hospital where I lend a hand sometimes, I heard a patient humming the Bosnian folk song "Azra." That song—which people in Bosnia like to sing, and which they consider to be a *sevdalinka,* a folk love dirge—was actually composed by an Austrian composer to the verses of Heinrich Heine, at the end of the last century.

There are many such songs, composed in Vienna to the verse of German and Austrian poets, that arrived in Bosnia with the Austrian administration. They were accepted as "Austrian *sevdalinkas,*" and people still sing them in Bosnia; they love them, believing that those songs speak about themselves and about their experience of the world. Bosnians know that those are not original, "genuine" *sevdalinkas,* but they love them, sing them, and consider them their own songs.

They are theirs, in fact, because they belong to Bosnia; they are images of Bosnia in the same way that another man's image of myself—my image in his eyes—belongs to me. It is true that my image in his eyes tells us about him, but it says something about me as well. It is true that his image of me belongs to him, but it does belong—in a way—to me, too.

Accordingly *sevdalinkas* imported to Bosnia from Austria

belong to nineteenth-century Austria, but they belong to Bosnia as well, in a way. These songs tell and show us how Austrian popular culture then perceived *sevdalinkas*, but they convey something about *sevdalinkas* themselves, because it is logical to presume that the viewer's image of the viewed depends on the nature of the viewed as well. At least a little bit.

Something very similar happened with what I like to call the pseudo-oriental style in architecture, which also arrived from Austria. That architectural style was accepted in Bosnia, and it still appears here and there—for instance when a wealthy man builds himself a house he wants to look "traditional," he builds it in the pseudo-oriental villa style, akin to the way that Austrians used to build their houses in Sarajevo and Mostar.

It is important to stress here that this architectural style did not jeopardize the traditional Bosnian style, just as Austrian *sevdalinkas* did not jeopardize their original Bosnian counterparts. The obvious differences between the "imports" and the "originals" were neither hidden nor diminished with time. This demonstrates that the openness of Bosnian culture to the complex influences of other cultures does not come from its lack of identity, or from its poor awareness of that identity, but from readiness to acknowledge the relevance and soundness of the attitudes of other cultures.

In other words, Bosnian culture has not accepted the "dictatorship of the subject"—a relationship in which one subject, say a person, defines another subject, strictly in its own terms—perhaps precisely because of its internal pluralism. My image in someone else's eyes depends both on him and me. What my interlocutor says is determined both by him and me. What I think and feel about someone else, depends both on him and me. The process of understanding does not occur between an active subject and a passive object, as though understanding were dependent on the subject alone.

In a culture composed of four co-equal monotheistic religions and their respective paradigms, it cannot be otherwise. In a cultural quartet, in which others repeatedly confirm me while I continuously confirm them, a "strong subject"—the one that turns everything it deals with into a passive object—is not possible.

That may explain my feeling of guilt after talking with the noble Frenchman. I felt truly guilty for not having suffered as much as it would suit my guest. How else could I feel, when I grew up in a cultural atmosphere that appreciates and accepts other views so much?

If it is his guest's belief that he is interminably unfortunate, a Bosnian finds it natural to accept this, as naturally as he expresses his love for Austrian *sevdalinkas*. I wonder whether I may be so unfortunate that I have lost sight of my own misfortune's dimensions, so that it appears to me that things are not all that bad after all.

But what about my dear guest from France being hurt by my refusal to be the victim to the degree he had planned for me? I did not want to hurt the man—I was honestly and deeply upset and tried hard to show the gratitude I felt with my whole being—and yet I have hurt him so deeply that we parted company almost in a rage.

Levi-Strauss says that a man sees in the world what his cultural system shows him and allows him to see—and Levi-Strauss is a Frenchman, as was that other gentleman who considered his own existence affirmed by his own thoughts. Can a man whose consciousness has been shaped by a monological culture allow the object he observes to influence his thinking? He cannot, of course.

Well, my guest from France observed me, but could not believe me, because he could not hear what I kept telling him. What was I talking about? In his view, the cause of my suffering lies in the fact that he thinks I suffer, because the fact of his thinking proves the fact of his existence, as the fact that he observes me and thinks about me proves that I exist. For him, I am a victim because he thinks that I am a victim, and so on...

We tried, we tried really hard. Yet we never understood each other. We could not help it; the differences between our cultures would not permit it. My culture—inherently pluralistic, polyphonous, dialogical; and his—inherently unitary, monological, homogeneous. My culture has embraced the Austrian *sevdalinkas* as its own; his is oblivious to all that its view does not encompass. And even right now, as I try to understand what happened then, I call upon you, my reader, to check whether I am right from your point of view. And he, the Frenchman, is sad, I suppose because of my ingratitude and unpreparedness to be as unhappy as he had suggested I should be—perhaps immeasurably sad, because his readiness to do good deeds is boundless.

So we are, without being responsible for it—far from each other, unable to understand each other, sad and locked up into our own respective circles. We do not blame each other, but we remain where we were when we parted ways. He, ready to do good deeds, and ending up misunderstood; and me, convinced the problem is that they are destroying my city only because there are the temples of four faiths in it.

I am sorry, truly sorry that my noble guest thinks I am ungrateful, but I also confess my sin of being even more sorry because my city is being destroyed, and because its temples are ever farther away from one another.

I could endure not having water and electricity, not having food and being cold—but how can I take the fact that I am being left forsaken in my own city? How can I believe in the unity and completeness of the world, if the world is being affirmed only in Jerusalem? How can I live if Jerusalem and I are alone, singular, shut inside our respective monologues? And how can I formulate this painful question to make it clear to my French friend as well?

LITERATURE AND WAR

I come from a destroyed country.

Fifteen years ago I would have considered an announcement like the one above impossible, or at least meaningless, if it were to be stated at the outset of a debate about literature. For I used to take seriously diverse formalisms, structuralisms, constructivisms, deconstructivisms, and numerous other isms that my schooling forced me to confront.

I took them seriously, believing that literature creates "pure" forms; that it has no connection with immediate reality; that what is being said is completely irrelevant, because only the way in which it is put forth matters; that content is a function of form, and that only as such does it become consequential. Theses about the content of an artistic creation seemed disgusting frauds of ideologized thought, worthless even for ridicule.

Working with my students and on my own texts, striving to understand literature from both outside and inside, I have become convinced that I was wrong, because literature indeed does have a lot to do with immediate reality, and is also greatly responsible for people's actions in immediate reality.

Literary work is constructed from two kinds of material: language and metalinguistic material. The latter includes feelings, thoughts, events, and aspects of character—the whole complex of factors affecting the character's actions, convictions, and world experience; the nature, flow, and internal logic of events that render their final outcome logical and necessary. The complex of factors that determine a character's behavior cannot be explained by their motivations alone.

Literary work is composed of material and form, content and function—all equally important and mutually determined; one could almost say that they create one another. Each of these dimensions of a literary work articulates its meanings and its values, or at least, thanks to the nature of aesthetic comprehension, determines the human experience of these values and, indirectly, determines human behavior in everday life. This shows that writing is related to the human experience of everyday reality and our actions in it.

Literature therefore dictates, or at least determines, our behavior through the values that culture imposes with an objective feeling that things make sense in the world. It also provides an instrument for interpretation of human experience in the world, and the reasons for our dwelling in it. The choices made within an accepted value system quite immediately determine human behavior, because the selection of values and the way we relate to them are the foundation of human ethical existence. These values and choices are most immediately articulated and determined by literature.

Different from other disciplines that create or articulate values, literature presents both the criteria for their selection and the values themselves, so that they seem to come from within, as individual human choices and experiences instead of appearing as external propositions.

Religion, for example, presents its values and choices for human beings as "divine propositions." Philosophy offers them in the form of rational comprehension and its consequences. Owing to the nature of aesthetic comprehension, literature comes closest to achieving an understanding that derives directly from experience. The Greek word *aisthesis* even means, among other things, understanding through experience, but this meaning is often overlooked for some reason.

Literature presents values and choices as entirely personal human experiences and as natural parts of being human, not results of a divine command or outcomes of a merely rational process. Because of that, we experience and defend the values brought into being by literature as essential to human existence, not as voluntary options; they are inner imperatives of our own beings, not requirements imposed by fate or knowledge.

What manifests itself here is the "pedagogical power" of literature, the power reckoned with by all sages (beginning with Plato) and rulers, ancient and modern. They all knew that literature shapes the cultural system and articulates values that the cultural system "assigns" to people who not only live in it, but who also comprehend and experience the world within the system's boundaries. Hence literature shapes human behavior and perception of the world, making selections from the value system that people use to give meaning to their existence.

That is why sages and rulers have strived to control literature and to create an unnatural relationship wherein literature would serve the purposes of politics, although their proper relationship is necessarily the exact opposite: Politics struggles to organize society so that the values created or articulated by literature can be realized in it. Politics can be, and is, an instrument of those disciplines that create values. The opposite relationship is contrary to nature, and therefore possible only for a short period of time, when the value-creating disciplines lose their real nature.

Literature is therefore doubtless responsible for politics, and to that extent one has to inquire about the responsibility and culpability that literature may have for some political forms, acts, and consequences. (Leaving aside the fact that no politics can entirely "realize" the system of values created by literature, and leaving aside the fact that, short of its impermissible violation, a very complex body of literary work cannot be reduced merely to a system of values that can be realized by any specific politics. These are themes that I have treated on several previous occasions.)*

The responsibility of literature became especially great after rationalism shattered the traditional unity of truth, good, and beauty, a unity that was relied upon until the advent of rationalism. In a world without unity, in a world where it is possible to create the atomic bomb and then decline any responsibility for it—as some of the atomic physicists on that glorious project did, invoking the ethical neutrality of the so-called pure sciences—literature remains the single defense and proof of the unity of the world and of human actions, pointing out that there are no neutral acts, that neutral acts are simply impossible. Religion does the same, by the way, but in a different fashion.

It is important to mention that this defense of the world's unity and of human wholeness is by no means a task assigned to literature from the outside. It is inherent to literature, which can be authentic only when it addresses complete human beings dwelling in an integrated world. To be true to itself literature must defend the integrity of the world and of the human being. Otherwise it ceases to be true literature and becomes the misuse of literary skill and craft.

Such misuses could not have been avoided, unfortunately, in a world without integrity and in a spiritual ambiance where

* The author's book *O jeziku i strahu* (*About Language and Fear*), published in Sarajevo in 1987, is entirely dedicated to this theme. It diagnosed the processes that ultimately led to the current war, and gained much favor among the independent intelligentsia of Belgrade, but this did not halt the nationalist indoctrination that was spreading at the time.

good, truth, and beauty are hopelessly separated. Since literature belongs among the most complex human activities, the
misuses of literature are more varied than misuses in other
areas of "spiritual work."They are no less detrimental, though,
taking into account the effect of literature in the real world.

There are numerous forms of misuse of the literary craft. I
would like to point out two of them that can rightfully be
held responsible for the initial statement of this chapter: I
come from a destroyed country. Bad literature, or misuse of
the literary craft, is responsible for that.

The first form of misuse of the literary craft I will speak
about is *l'art pour l'art*—art for art's sake, if you will. It appears
with various "vanguards," experimental literary projects, and,
of course, hand in hand with the struggle for the freedom of
literature. In that struggle, it is most important to prove that
literary work has no content, and that the metalinguistic
material is utterly irrelevant, because literature—like any
other art—is a "pure form."

By depriving literary work of its content, and by divesting
metalinguistic material of all meaning, the authors of such
literature reduce their craft to a series of processes that result
in a literary form. Within that context, processes have practi-
cally nothing to do with the material that is being shaped by
them. The processes used to create a literary form are reduced
to a self-contained game that does not point to anything
beyond itself. In the past, the process of developing and
molding material was the sacred secret of any serious trade.
Now it is a game enclosed in itself, like an enigmatic witti-
cism or a children's puzzle.

It is entirely normal for writers of this literature to opt for the so-called subliterary genres, where metalinguistic material comes as a given, in advance, as a rule. In this case, literary skill is exhausted in the construction of a recognizable form with an odd "surprise." I am thinking of potboilers, books written with the sole ambition of achieving commercial success, and others that aspire to belong to purportedly "higher" literature yet employ irony as no more than a clever gadget.

It is also entirely normal to justify this "selection of genre" with irony: firstly with irony vis-à-vis the "traditional notion of literature"; after that with irony vis-à-vis the world and the very notion of meaning; and then with irony vis-à-vis the rules and forms of the genre that authors of ironic literature keep on producing.

It is also entirely unsurprising that the prevalence of this orientation in literature brought about the long dreamed-of absolute freedom of literature. This kind of literature is truly adorned with an absolute freedom, because nobody orders anything from it, nobody persecutes it, nobody imputes anything to it, and there are no intentional misreadings of it—because there is no reason for any such thing.

Who could mind or need a self-contained game of processes that mold pseudo-literary material? This game produces itself alone, and incidentally causes a naive reader to thrill to the recognition of familiar things, and produces indifference to what happens outside of this literature, in the material world, or the role that literature may have in it.

Perhaps this indifference explains the absolute freedom that literature enjoys in the supposedly modern, democratic, and free world. The measure of freedom that the writer enjoys in the contemporary world (as well as the measure of freedom from responsibility that this absolute freedom presumes) has not been given to the sick, the absolutist rulers, or to the children. It is the right to do entirely what one wants, while engaging in one's craft and earning daily bread.

Doctors, bakers, carpenters, or engineers, telephone operators, miners, policemen, and students—all of them are obliged to respect the basic rules of their respective crafts, and to preserve the integrity of those enterprises. For no sane person would consider living in an experimental house or wearing an ironic suit (with the exception of the emperor in his new clothes). Only a writer has no obligations to his craft, and has no reason to preserve its integrity and logic, or to respect obligations that his craft assigns to him.

This indifference perhaps explains the fact that contemporary rulers have no problems with unfettered literature, because they have no interest in it, while their predecessors carefully watched over it—although few of today's leaders have ever read Plato's views on the pedagogical power of literature.

Literature completely liberated itself from the rulers' custody after it won its freedom to be an arbitrary game, a little bit more than nothing, that produces nothing else but the joy of recognition and indifference. And indeed, why should rulers pay attention to arbitrary games? Why should they watch carefully over indifference? Well, much more meaning and challenging of destiny are involved in going out into the street—a person can be knocked on the head by a falling shingle, or meet the woman dearest to his heart. It is riskier to board a streetcar—one can run into a young bully mistreating a lady. It is even more dangerous to shake hands—the other person could have some infection—than to write a book reduced to literary games. Such literature has truly won an absolute freedom—and it can have it.

It may be that the indifference produced and accommodated by such literature also explains the frightening degree of artlessness shown by many contemporary writers. It would be worrisome in a child, because it might indicate mental retardation. Those writers are confused by the world (which is not strange, or at least would not be strange if they would not demonstrate it so conspicuously), and in the best of cases they react to all that happens around them with a single question: Could this be used for an interesting narrative twist?

In their experience, literature, the world, and they themselves are completely free from any ethical questions—which is a normal consequence of the reduction of literature to play, and of turning ethical questions into aesthetic ones. Those people have forgotten the very word *good*—be it in terms of adequacy within literature itself, or as an issue in life.

How is this kind of literature responsible for the fact that I come from a destroyed country?

It is responsible indirectly, by transgressing against the fundamental rules of its craft and its integrity, and thus contributing—as much as it could, and that was a lot—to the spreading of general indifference in an indifferent world. For, let us not fool ourselves: the world is written first—the holy books say that it was created in words—and all that happens in it, happens in language first.

An event in language precedes events in the world, which means that the universal indifference of the world started from language, from writing, from literature that has liberated itself by removing its meaning and sense, reasons and value, reducing itself to an arbitrary game.

The indifference of people prepared to do anything in order to feel something, to really feel something—at least momentarily—started with an art whose practitioners decided to liberate it, and thus discovered the daring beauty of the totally senseless game. The indifference of the world originated in an "indifferent art" that has aestheticized its ethical component. In the name of the beauty of outrageousness, that art completely abdicated its ethical responsibility and integrity, which are the unavoidable obligations of every craft.

The practitioners of that art have decided not to produce sense and meaning but to offer its user a "surprise" instead of a partial identification with a fictitious world; an identification that would make possible a fuller comprehension and understanding of one's own self, through a temporary sojourn with an Other—one which makes it possible to live one's own existence more fully after having experienced the existence of an Other.

People who observe and experience the most horrendous suffering of their neighbors as a mere aesthetic excitement; people who aestheticize death and agree to watch the worst torments in order to feel something—for a moment at least—such people are inscribed in contemporary literature, which is entirely free and pure, written by authors with a surplus of artlessness.

That is the guilt of this art-for-art's-sake literature, which is indirectly responsible for all the horrors of the contemporary world, including the horrors taking place in my country right now. The decision to perceive literally everything as an aesthetic phenomenon—completely sidestepping questions about goodness and the truth—is an artistic decision. That decision started in the realm of art, and went on to become characteristic of the contemporary world.

People who watch violence and the worst suffering in order to feel something for a moment are the aestheticized people produced by contemporary indifferent art. Here lies the guilt of literature that I spoke about—skillful, well-written, and indifferent—a self-contained game of a renegade literary craft that has forgotten that the process of molding must proceed from the properties of the material.

The second misuse of the literary craft is not so indirect but is immediate instead. Its guilt is obvious and incalculable, but unfortunately unavoidable and so enormous that it cannot be overlooked. I am thinking about literature with prophetic ambitions, and about the use of literature for political goals. That literature, while seeming to preserve the integrity of its craft, uses it, nevertheless, to produce followers instead of to clarify ideas. In other words, literature is used to create and impose faulty values.

If the first misuse of literature can be somewhat precisely denoted as art-for-art's-sake, this one can be defined, with the same measure of (im)precision, as "heroic" literature. What is it about?

This literature preserves the integrity of its craft and

seemingly respects all its rules. It actually respects all the rules except the fundamental one—that a craft must not be used for evil. In the past, professional status in a craft was granted upon the recommendation of the master, who had to attest to the ethical maturity of the candidate; the recommendation was his personal responsibility, precisely because of the possibility of a skill being used for evil.

Training in a skill did not encompass a mere mastery of the technical procedures required by the craft but included ethical training as well. A candidate could not receive a title if his ethical standards did not ensure that he would use his skills for good—regardless of his possibly superior technical knowledge of the craft.

From the literary-critical point of view, "heroic" literature is an interesting combination of realism from the last century and medieval literature. The technical process of treating the metalinguistic material links it to nineteenth-century realism; the principles of selection, and the kind of material chosen, link it to medieval literature.

As in the realistic literature of the past century, the narration is logically arranged and motivated; characters are constituted as relatively complete systems with rather clearly defined characteristics, from which their acts logically follow; motivational systems are complete and well ordered.

What makes this kind of literature different from the realistic literature of the past century, which makes it akin to medieval literature, are precisely its characters, who are never simply one character, a single destiny, or a protagonist of a single event. Usually they are representatives of some community, of something wider and more important than the character itself, a concrete manifestation of a certain paradigm.

In medieval literature that place was occupied by the religious community or a social group, of course—as in the case of stories about knights—while in the "heroic" literature I am talking about the paradigm is a nation or a political party. People in this literature are Serbs, Croats, Communists, Royalists, or something similar in the first place. Only after that, in the second or third place, are they people with personal traits.

This logic, so typical of medieval literature—both dramatic and prose—is plainly visible in the motivational mechanisms of the stories. Namely, the hero's destiny in this kind of literature does not reside in his character, but in the group he belongs to, because both his actions and his future depend much more on where he belongs than on what kind of person he is.

In all novels of chivalry, a knight must act in accord with the knightly ideal: He has to practice "courtly manners" and fight bravely when he confronts demons, like Yvain in the romance *The Knight and the Lion* by the twelfth-century writer Chrétien de Troyes. A believer must similarly repent after a grave sin, even if he has sold his soul to the Evil One, like Theophil, the unfortunate predecessor of Faust.

In this heroic literature, group identification determines destiny and actions, while individual human identity—the total of recognizable individual traits—is just an incidental phenomenon. Moreover, identity is a consequence of belonging to a group, as both medieval and contemporary authors of this kind of literature would say.

Both in this literature and in its medieval counterpart,

whatever happens to a person happens because he is a Serb or a Communist, and not because he is himself. Furthermore, he does what he does, he acts the way he acts, because he is a Serb—he even loves his wife the way he does because he is a Serb or a Communist, and so on.

This last proposition should be argued with one serious reservation, because the authors I am talking about are not too adroit when it comes to portraying female characters and love episodes, perhaps because a female character creates many more problems, and demands far more refinement, than that necessary for heroically masculine simplifications.

What do we get as a result of the mixture of motivations commonly found in medieval literature, and those characteristic of the literature of psychological realism? We get precisely the literary bastard I am talking about—literature in which a character feels, desires, breathes, and thinks in accord with the group to which he belongs.

Medieval literary personages are not individualized. They are emphatically typified and paradigmatic, because the medieval literary perspective is external to the character, so that a novel or a drama simply registers his acts. The character himself simply accomplishes his task, as is proper for such literature: a knight acts the way he does because he is obliged to act out certain behavior according to the ideal he represents; a believer acts the way he does because God's will is above his; it is stronger and superimposed on his will.

It is possible that a character's acts happen to be contrary to his individual desires, which is what happened to the knight in Chrétien de Troyes's romance. He lay wounded in the Dark Knight's castle, where he fell in love with his host's wife. Ultimately, however, he renounced his love in the name of an ideal. Then there was Tristan and Isolde, who did not exactly hold back, by the way—but that was because of that damned love potion.

In the literature of psychological realism, which is where this literary bastard gets its motivational technique, character is greatly individualized and the narrative's perspective is placed within it. Because of that, equal attention is paid to what the hero feels, desires, and wants, and to what he does. In the same way, characters in this bastard literature individually feel, desire, think, and want to identify with the group to which they belong.

Should we emphasize that in this way a character simply renders in concrete form or embodies the collective to which the hero belongs, which then appears as a paradigm? This motivational technique sanctifies the collective, which begins to function in the same way that divinity used to function in medieval literature: character is completely saturated with the character of the collective it belongs to, and is at the same time contained totally within the collective.

In this literature—which I mention as an example of the misuse of the literary craft for the creation of faulty values—the political community appears as God and belonging to the political community looks like destiny. There are no feelings, no wishes, no thoughts, and no acts beyond belonging to the political community. Destiny lies within that belonging, and anything that a human being can have within, around, above him- or herself, or anywhere else—is within that political community.

This motivational system is neatly combined with topics that are, once again, a bastardized amalgam of principles used to construct topics characteristic of medieval literature, blended with topics characteristic of the realistic literature from the past century.

On one hand, the topic is always the suffering of the character because of his political affiliation. That can happen because he rebelled against the collective he belonged to—in the way a sinner in medieval literature rebels against God—or because the others, the enemies, punish him for belonging to that collective—as they punished the captured crusader whom death did not want in the *Miracles of Saint Nicholas*.

On the other hand, the topic is constructed as a series of entirely individual acts and events that logically follow from one another. This usually produces a literary bastard, in which the martyr's role is articulated as a series of individual decisions and acts although the appearance of free will is really a charade.

This is how we have arrived at a literature that presents the collective as divine, and belonging to that collective as the highest possible value, worth even more than a human being who as an individual desires, or wants, believes, dreams, or understands.

The human being is worthless as an individual; he has to overcome all that is personal in himself, and become completely immersed in the collective that saturates and contains an individual totally. That transcendence of the individual must be the individual's own decision, just as it is his destiny. Many of our novels and inspirational poems testify to that.

The transcendence of one's own self is a heroic act of surrender, by means of which a human being becomes himself and the collective simultaneously—comparable to those heroes that were the fruit of love between pagan gods and mortal women. They are human and divine beings in one, which is why this literary bastard is called "heroic" literature.

The betrayal of human individuality and transgression of human standards are fundamental sins in all normal times. In Greek tragedies there was the Chorus, which set limits on what is human and witnessed the great sin of hubris by those who wanted to step beyond those limits. Already there in that fundamental sin, the creation of faulty values in this type of literature, and its assistance in the service of evil, begins.

One *hadis** says that it is a fundamental sin to say that there is no God, and that a man who utters that statement is capable of doing anything. The same rule applies: after having committed a fundamental sin, this literature behaves as if it is allowed to do anything. And so it calls upon people to burn children to death (Djura Jaksić†); it creates a mother who offers to a revolution that had already taken three of her sons as many more sons as it might need (Skender Kulenović‡); it calls for a final showdown with people of a different faith, or explains that all evil that befalls a collec-

---

* One of the two literary sources of Islam, the other one being the Koran, of course. An Arabic word, *hadis* means "sayings" or "traditions" concerning Muhammad.

† The author refers to these lines from the many works by this popular Serb poet: "Die brothers! Wade in blood! Let the villages burn! Into the flames throw children alive!"

‡ The author refers to the poem "Stojanka, Mother of Knezopolje" by this well-known Bosnian-Herzegovinian Communist writer.

tive comes from another collective (Slobodan Selenić*).

There is no use wasting any words on the complete opus of Dobrica Cosić, Antonije Isaković†, and a whole series of other writers, because they are obvious examples of what I am talking about, needing no explanation.

I am talking about a specific type of misuse of literature, whereby the literary craft is being used for the production of evil. If the first misuse I talked about is a crime, being an act against humanity, this second type of misuse of my craft can only be described as a sin. It is literally a crime against dear God because it ascribes the attributes of divinity to the mute, shapeless collective that interposes itself vis-à-vis human beings in a position that God alone can occupy.

Because of that literature—and in the name of the values it has created, articulated, and imposed—the cities burn now, children become invalids, everything human is being destroyed, debased, and annulled. Because of that literature they now forcibly impregnate women, which not only humiliates them personally and debases their capacity to be mothers, but degrades even that sublime gift of the woman to objectify, to embody, to show love as the highest form of relationship between two people, by giving birth to the fruit of love.

---

* The author refers to the novel *Timor Mortis* by this influential Serb writer, the last chair of the Writers' Guild of the former Yugoslavia.

† Dobrica Cosić is the most widely read of all living Serb writers, president of Yugoslavia (Serbia-Montenegro) in 1992–1993 and was ousted by the hardline Serb nationalists in the present Yugoslav Parliament. He is often called the father of the present-day Serb nationalist revival. His works include the fiction cycle "Time of Death" and a book of essays, *The Real and the Possible.* Antonije Isaković is a politically influential Serb writer. Note that he has a family name virtually identical with that of Isa Bey Ishakovic, the founder of Sarajevo, who, ironically, might have been a medieval Serb convert to Islam.

And people who burn down the cities, maim the children, and impregnate women by force—they are inspired, directly or indirectly, by the literature I am talking about. Directly, if they have read it, or indirectly, if they have not read it but have appropriated the values that this literature has created. Because of this literature I come from a destroyed country.

But why am I really saying all this? Well, these things are well known, because the leaders of the Serb nationalistic parties who have destroyed Yugoslavia and pushed it into war have all been profoundly influenced by writers and professors of literature. Even the political platform of today's Serbia (the Memorandum of 1986) was written by the Serbian Academy of Arts and Sciences, whose membership includes dozens of writers and professors of literature. And it is generally understood that, once this war is over, they will wearily refute responsibility in the manner of sages dedicated to higher matters, because they are above all writers, for God's sake.

But I am not talking about them, I am talking about literature. I am not interested in their personal guilt (God will surely judge them, and perhaps even honorable people before that), but in the culpability of my craft, the craft I cannot practice anymore, before answering some questions.

We persistently avoid those questions, acting like Sleeping Beauties who dream about pure form, the beauty of the beyond and similar esoteric inventions, believing that we will never be awakened by a prince red with children's blood. Those are the questions I have to answer before I am able to continue the work I have to do.

What is my responsibility in all this? What is it that I could have and should have done to diminish those horrors but have failed to do? What have I done to contribute to all that is happening? Yes, I am responsible, I am a colleague of those people, we share the same language and trade, I even know some of them personally. So, I could not be completely innocent.

I have discovered one of my mistakes while speaking about the first form of the misuse of literature: I was indifferent, I took seriously the freedom of literature, which is actually free only because it is mistakenly regarded as being insignificant. I discover my second mistake right now, as I write down the characteristics that transform literature with prophetic ambitions into a silly and sad literary bastard.

Maybe one of those who slaughters people now would be quietly sitting somewhere instead if I had cautioned him in time about the kind of literature it is that he admires. Would that be all, however? Would it be that my craft and I are only a little bit guilty? Let us not forget that the world has been written down first, then spoken, and only after that did it come into being materially. And let us also not forget that I come from a destroyed country. God, how I wish I could forget that—even if only for a moment?

City Portraits

HOTEL EUROPA

THE HOTEL EUROPA IS THE PHYSICAL AND SEMAN-
tic center of the city of Sarajevo. It is the physical
center because it sits exactly on the border between
the Turkish and Austro-Hungarian parts of the city—at the
precise midpoint of what Sarajevo truly is. This hotel embodies the foundation of the city's identity: that combination of
facts and traits linked with its name.* Sarajevo is a blending of
Turkish and Austro-Hungarian history and culture—of Ori-
ent and Occident—in a specific balance of quality and quan-
tity. Everything else that makes up Sarajevo—everything that
was built after the decline of the Austro-Hungarian empire—
is not a city but a mere collection of buildings.

It is even more plain that the Hotel Europa is the semantic
center of Sarajevo. It was built at the edge of the Turkish part
of the city, on the borderline dividing it from the Austrian
part. By "borderline," I mean a place that is sumultaneously
inside and outside, a place that belongs to what it delineates
while remaining altogether something else. With the Hotel
Europa two epochs and two faces of Sarajevo meet, and
touch, and complement one another. The Europa is their
mutual borderline, a place that belongs to one and to the
other, at the same time, while remaining beyond both.

---

* The first part of the name descends from Turkish and Persian sources; that is,
serai, which means an inn, a mansion, or a palace. There is even an alternative
spelling of the name, *Serajevo*. This same root is discovered in the English word,
caravanserai, or caravansary, a place where a caravan stops to rest during a long
journey. Sarajevo thus sadly, ironically, means a resting place, a place where a weary
traveler can find shelter and rest before commencing on the next leg of a long
and difficult journey.

The Turkish part of the city ends with the Europa. With its pseudo-Turkish style, through which imperial Austria tried to make itself feel at home in Sarajevo, the Europa belongs to the Turkish part of the city as the reflection of an object in a funhouse mirror belongs to that object. In the same manner, Austrian *sevdalinkas*, for example, composed in Vienna to the verses of Germanic poets—long forgotten in Austria but still loved in Bosnia—belong to Bosnia.

The hotel belongs to the Turkish quarter in the same way that the image of ourselves in the gaze of another belongs to us; it is an image that speaks equally about the Other and about ourselves. The Europa also belongs to the Turkish part of the city because of the naive pictures with Oriental motifs on its walls; the imitation Oriental carpets on its floors; and the fact that its restaurant and its dining room are hidden deep within it, as in Bosnian houses. Yes, the Europa belongs to the Turkish part of the city in all those ways in which the image of our own being in the gaze of another person truly belongs to ourselves.

The Austrian part of the city begins with the Europa, which belongs to Austria because of its name, by its internal organization, and by the nationality of those who have built it. The Europa is the first Central European hotel in this part of the world, and it is the purest example of Central European culture in Sarajevo. When I say Central Europe, I speak of an abundance of small ethnic groups used to living in mutual tolerance, integration, and protection of the other's identity—which is a confirmation of one's own identity when you recognize it. Those groups were accustomed to living together in the same way that Middle Eastern and Central European elements mingle in the decor of the Hotel Europa.

When I say Central Europe I also speak of the feeling that culture is—above all else—a way of living, a quiet shaping of the days and human ambiance, not pretentious epochal projects and "cosmic systems." I also speak of a distinctly humorous attitude toward ourselves and the world, an attitude that creates a distance from ourselves and promotes tolerance and respect for others.

The Hotel Europa is therefore the semantic center of Sarajevo. Bearing elements of both the East and of Central Europe, this hotel is like a prism that gathers within itself the diffuse rays of what Sarajevo truly is. I know that one cannot say what the "Sarajevan spirit" or the "identity of Sarajevo" is, because it cannot be defined, although it can be learned aesthetically, through experience. Hence one goes to the Hotel Europa for a cake or an ice cream, not because of the cakes (which are, to be honest, much better elsewhere), but because of the Hotel Europa, where Sarajevo can be felt with one's fingertips, where it can be smelled and sensed. It is first felt within, experientially, as a part of ourselves, and then understood. To know Sarajevo means to need to go to the Hotel Europa quite regularly.

Late in July 1992 the Hotel Europa, which housed refugee women and children, was set aflame by an artillery projectile. The next projectile killed five of those Sarajevans who were trying to extinguish the blaze and save their hotel.

SARAJEVO'S JEWS—ONE MORE EXODUS

The Jews came to Sarajevo in the beginning of the six-
teenth century, after Ferdinand and Isabella had banished
them from the newly conquered Spanish lands. These
were our Sephardim, who brought with them the Spanish
language and *Ladino,** as well as the Hebrew faith and culture,
their memories of the long centuries of wandering, and
a feeling—deeper by far than consciousness, because it
presupposes a readiness, a perfect promptitude to act—that
migration is the genuine human condition in this world.
Besides all that, they brought some practical skills that were
scarce in Sarajevo before their arrival.

They settled in Byelave, until then an uninhabited hill,
which later became a full-fledged *mahala* of its own. Then as
now, that district was synonymous with poverty and life in a
tightly knit community whose members helped each other.
Yet Byelave ceased to be an exclusively Jewish *mahala*, just as
poverty ceased to be the most important trait of Sarajevo's
Jews. The Sephardim had also long ceased to be the only Jews
in Sarajevo. After their large and enormously significant
period of immigration, several waves of Ashkenazic Jews
reached the city from the north, bringing new languages and
new customs, new forms of culture, and the everlasting Jewish feeling that migration is a natural human condition.

---

* As Yiddish was a blend of Hebrew and German, and widely spoken by
Ashkenazic Jews throughout Eastern Europe, Ladino was an amalgam of Hebrew
and Spanish, and was widely spoken by Sephardic Jews throughout
the Mediterranean world, the Balkans, and the Levant.

The impact of the Jewish arrival was immediate, not only because of the new languages, new customs, and the new people, but also because of the ability of these new Sarajevans to work and to earn, to prosper and to build homes for themselves as well as to help in building the city for everyone's benefit. Very soon after the Sephardim arrived, there were enough wealthy Jews in Sarajevo to make their presence strongly felt in business and in the general life of the city. As their wealth grew, their numbers rose, and their graveyard expanded on a wonderful hill some two kilometers beyond the extreme limits of the city, marked at that time by the Magribiya mosque, on the western edge of town.

I can still remember the names that I encountered first at that graveyard, and then again in the catalogue of a great exhibition on the architecture of Bosnia and Herzegovina from the period of 1878–1914:* Daniel A. Salom, Samuel Sumbulovic, Josef Zadik Danon, Avram Zadik Danon, Josef Sabetaj Finci, Mordohaj Atijas, Izidor Izrael, Aron Musafija....These are the names of men who financed the construction of the big apartment and commercial buildings that are an inescapable part of the physiognomy of Sarajevo, names that adorned some of the tombstones in the great Jewish graveyard, one of the places I was acquainted with and learned to love immediately after moving to Sarajevo in 1972.

There is something fascinating about the Jewish graveyard.

---

* By the decision of the Berlin Congress of 1878, Bosnia and Herzegovina were occupied by Austria-Hungary. World War I started in 1914, ending the Austrian-Hungarian architectural input in the region. Four years later, Bosnia and Herzegovina joined the newly founded Kingdom of the Serbs, Croats, and Slovenes, renamed Yugoslavia in 1929.

It is not like the Muslim cemeteries in Sarajevo, which do not have the atmosphere of a graveyard because they look more like gardens; they are popular local parks, quite naturally and normally open to everybody. The Jewish graveyard looks like a graveyard; it has a graveyard atmosphere, too, and yet it remains a place where the young people of Sarajevo often meet, where they set off for a stroll and a cigarette. I know some couples who have exchanged their first kisses right there, in the Jewish graveyard.

Why is it so? How is it possible that a place that is in every respect a graveyard—and whose every feature reminds you of that fact—nevertheless became integrated with city life for several generations? I thought about this question a lot (perhaps because I often walk to the Jewish graveyard for its beautiful view of the Austro-Hungarian part of Sarajevo, and to have a smoke), and I talked about it with several people, but we could find no answer. It simply is so. The Jewish graveyard is simply a place we Sarajevans walk to gladly, a place that we have in many little ways subtly merged with our lives, making it a part of our daily existence.

In April 1992 the Jewish graveyard became involved in our deaths as well. The snipers of the Yugoslav People's Army opened precise and deadly fire upon Sarajevo's citizens from the graveyard hill. Is that proper and just? And in accordance with what principles, if it is?

I know that it happened in accordance with the same principles that caused the attack on Sarajevo to begin precisely in the year of our Jewish community's observance of its 500th anniversary of their exile from Spain. Half a millennium of

common life was observed in the encircled city, semi-destroyed {95}
and surrounded by heavy artillery, so that not even a bird could
enter. Yet it was commemorated decorously and sadly, in the
only way the anniversary of an exile can be observed.

I was thinking—during those days when all of us were
deeply shaken, moving around the city with tears in our eyes,
less watchful of the cannon shells than normally—that even
in normal conditions the "celebration" of such a jubilee necessarily contains something hollow. But now, I thought, my
God, why does it cast such shadows on our future? Why do
we all suspect and feel acutely—in flashes at least—that this
observance bears something portentous and all too painful?

I would have liked it better if we had commemorated this
year less well, even if that commemoration had turned out to
be less beautiful and less dear to us all. We commemorated as
we did, however—in a semi-destroyed city caught up,
besieged so tightly that not even a bird could fly in or out—in
a city caught up in such a fate just because its inhabitants
wanted to live together, with all their differences in faiths,
languages, and cultures.

Everything became unraveled less than twenty days after
that commemoration, where many a nice word was spoken
and even a few solemn oaths were given: Less than twenty days
after that observance nearly the entire Jewish community left
the city, heading for a new exile. Perhaps ten odd fanatical
lovers of their homes and the city stayed on. The same principles that involved our Jewish graveyard in our deaths for the
first time, the same laws that willed our Jews to commemorate
five hundred years of exile, the same laws that caused their city

to disappear gradually in front of their very eyes—these laws caused Sarajevo to be left virtually without its Jews, the community whose arrival made Sarajevo a complete world in miniature, the planet's little heart, and the community that profoundly determined the city's physiognomy.

I saw our Jews off, wishing them good luck with a painful lump in my throat, with a dying breath in my soul, and a feeling that something most wonderful ended on that day, forever.

That same day I remembered a story that my old friend Albert Goldstein told me to explain why he would not move to Israel, and why he thinks that the world Jewish community splits into Israelis and Jews:

> For two thousand years now, on the eve of our greatest holiday, my ancestors have repeated this sentence: 'Next year in Jerusalem.' That sentence preserved them; that sentence is the vertical axis of their experience of the world and their place in it; that sentence is an unavoidable part of our identity. Spoken in the city of Jerusalem itself, it simply makes no sense. And it is stupid to renounce a two-thousand-year-long dream, to renounce one's own identity, for the sake of a certain number of buildings that make up the real city of Jerusalem.

Thus spoke my friend Albert Goldstein—eloquently, wisely, and wittily. Perhaps truthfully as well, yet that truth— if it is tangibly experienced—hurts like the devil.

Late in the night of the day when we saw our Jews off, I felt—with an ache that took my breath away—that my city had already moved toward the imaginary quarters where Goldstein's Jewish Jerusalem dwelled for two thousand years, at the very center of the world. Behind lowered eyelashes I saw

Sarajevo, so much ruined and so much loved—loved as never before—rising up from the earth, taking off and flying away, somewhere beyond, where everything is gentle and tranquil. It flew toward the deepest recesses of reality, where it can be loved and dreamed about, and from where it can shine back upon us, rich with meaning, like a beckoning destination.

Does this mean, oh my God, that I have already given this Sarajevo up? Does it mean that Sarajevo as I know it and love it does not exist anymore? Does it mean—if it is Thy will that it should so happen—that it was too good and too beautiful for this world, which does not seem to be altogether worthy of Thee, its Creator? Shall we indeed, my fellow citizens and I, on the eve of every holiday, when the day that we wish to be beautiful is about to begin, repeat as a dream, as an oath, and as a prayer: "Next year in Sarajevo"—for the next five thousand years? And in the meantime, Sarajevo will shine down on us, ever farther away from us and from this world.

Letters Among Friends

The letter that follows is an integral part of the book *Dnevnik selidbe* (*Sarajevo, Exodus of a City*), and one of its sources, because my first thought of leaving Sarajevo sprang from it. On the day when I received this letter from my friend, the original publisher of this book, the drama of my move started; all that came afterward was simply a technical execution of it. In Sarajevo, everything was clear, clean, and terrible; there was no longer drama in Sarajevo; upon leaving Sarajevo, I understood that I could not remain innocent, because I had to betray either Sarajevo and myself, by remaining outside, or my fundamental calling, by returning. My situation would not permit ethically nonambiguous acts. Once I understood the dimensions of the tragedy that had struck the people of Bosnia, I realized that my choice, whatever it turned out to be, would be a faulty one. I think this is one of the fateful results of the war that Serbia started against Croatia and Bosnia—the fact that ethically nonambiguous acts became impossible for us, the attacked ones. Following the ideas of his letter and moving away from my destined place, I stepped into the space of a drama whose contours and dimensions I strive to describe with this book.

LETTER FROM N.

Zagreb, December 27, 1992

Dear Dzevad,

I will not write what you and Dragana already know, I hope: that we are thinking about you all the time. We are not even worrying anymore, like we did in the beginning; we are living with you as our everyday companions, instead. We will talk about that face to face; there is no sense in writing about it.

At this moment, it is most important for you to get out of Sarajevo and to write, speak, and testify. Two or three times a week they call me from Germany, Austria, and France, asking about your writings, about the possibility of you appearing there in person. This has fallen upon all of us, in a way, as a duty. Nobody believes anything the politicians are saying; they want to hear and read writers. Furthermore, with writers like Cosic, you must be heard from. The political influence that we, the so-called intellectuals, have among the humanitarian organizations and some important people abroad who make decisions in politics, is very big, and most often results in immediate aid to the people. As you have a novel, and a full European background in theory, don't waste a single moment. *Hereby I extend an open invitation from your German colleagues for your appearance in Berlin and Hamburg, on the 18 and 19 of February; the same goes for Graz, Klagenfurt, and Vienna, at the beginning of March. I am authorized to do this by the Literaturhaus of Berlin, Forum Stadtpark, and the publisher Alois Wieser, in the name of the cultural authorities of the provincial and municipal administration.* Take Dragana as well, if you can, or let her come later on; I spoke about her to everybody, so all invitations are valid for her, too. In technical terms, your base will initially be in Zagreb (you will live with me at first, because we have a separate room with a bathroom): there are arrangements for a grant in Klagenfurt later on, where everybody speaks Slovenian and, by God, even Croatian. *You, Dzevad, must become an ambassador of your people.* Bosnia has nobody abroad, while you and Dragana have all the qualifications. Until you move out, get hold of a fax machine and send some articles; they are ordered from me by *Die Zeit* (Martin, do you remember him?), *Frankfurter Rundschau* (Roman).* *Taz* from Berlin, then *Esprit* from Paris, two papers from Vienna, and *Estado de São Paulo.* But understand this: after that, people will want to talk to you even more.

Write essays, prepare as many materials as you can, from others as well, if you don't have enough of your own. This is not marketing, don't think that, the issue is tens of thousands of Bosnian children and women who wander around Europe, and nobody dares to ask them anything, nor can they explain anything to anybody. You are the ones who can be articulate. There were demonstrations for an intervention the other day in Paris; they are preparing new ones, but our colleagues need argumentation. You can give that a hundred times better than Berti, myself, or Jancar.†

Divan is now with the publisher, Wieser of Klagenfurt; Egmont‡ had no money to print and bind it (20,000 Deutschmarks). I am writing in a hurry; Berti has let me know that it is possible to take the letter tomorrow. Be smart and lis-

---

* Martin Klingst, a journalist, with *Die Zeit.* Roman Arens, an independent journalist who became the Italian correspondent of the *Frankfurter Rundschau.*

† Berti is the nickname of Albert Goldstein, the author's longtime friend, then writing and publishing from Zagreb. Jancar is Drago Jancar, a writer from Ljubljana.

‡ *The Eastern Divan* is the author's latest completed novel, published in Sarajevo in 1989. Egmont is Egmont Hesse, poet and publisher of the Galrev Verlag of Berlin.

ten to older people! Military planes are taking off for Sarajevo from here every day, so you can return at any moment, if you become aware that you are more needed in Sarajevo than here. We shall fix that through our terrific connections.

Nenad*

Kiss Dragana.

A BELATED REPLY TO N.

Dear Nenad,
I received your letter through a friend who worked in the Sarajevo hospital where I used to help out. I followed your advice. I left Sarajevo on Thursday, February 27, 1993, around 5 P.M., two months to the day after your last letter to me. As you urged me to, I have written as much as I could. I have spoken out often. I have struggled to explain to the people from the so-called West all that has transpired in our old country. I have strived to articulate the horror that has rendered my countrymen speechless. I was grateful before I left Sarajevo, and I am still grateful for all the expressions of friendship on your part, for all the truly precious conversations, for all the sensitivity you have expressed to me personally and toward the tragedy of Bosnia and the Bosnians. As you must also know, I will never forgive you for having been so damn right; nor will I ever forgive myself for heeding your advice.

Even before the war, even in the best of times, I found it difficult to endure life and the beautiful world of God (you might

---

* Nenad Popovic (author of this letter) is a writer, translator, and the publisher of Durieux, in Zagreb, Croatia, the original publisher of *Sarajevo, Exodus of a City* (*Dnevnik selidbe*) .

have sensed something of the kind from my writings, and you might have heard about it from the people who are close to me). I endured them (life and the beautiful world) thanks to illusions, to art, to my confidence in meaning, in the human need for truth, and in the human dedication to the good.

These things helped me to withstand the war in Sarajevo as well: I believed at first, like other Sarajevans, that the "free world" would not permit an unwarranted slaughter of us civilians; later on I believed, like other Sarajevans, that the world permits the slaughter of civilians only because it does not yet understand and does not yet know what is happening in our old country. Because of these beliefs I took heed of your letter. I left Sarajevo and spent a year writing, speaking, explaining, believing—like yourself—that the main problem is just a lack of understanding and inadequate information.

I kept repeating, ad nauseum, that the war in Bosnia is not a civil war but a slaughter, because while a war is possible between armies, in Bosnia we have an attack of the "Yugoslav People's Army" on civilians; I pleaded that the idea there are "three sides in the conflict" is wrong because it overlooks the most numerous "fourth side"—the Bosnian population, which prefers integration, tolerance, and a Bosnian multicultural community; I repeated that women who were imprisoned in the Chetnik camps were not just raped but forcibly and deliberately impregnated, and I explained the critical difference between rape and forced impregnation, in which a woman is made to bear an unwanted child. I did that for a year, dear friend, explaining, repeating, and in the end understood that I was performing a futile task.

All our efforts to explain (yours as well as mine) are futile, simply because the issue is not the lack of understanding or inadequate information but a deliberately false naming of things. No serious person can really believe that we are truly dealing with a civil war here, or that the forced impregnation of a woman is the same thing as rape, as awful as that crime is. Western politicians are much better informed than we are, and they know, down to the tiniest detail, what is happening (Presidents Mitterand and Bush had evidence showing the existence of Chetnik concentration camps in July of 1992). They deliberately give false names to things in order to distort those very things, to "justify" their own ineptness, forlornness, passiveness, and indecisiveness. I finally realize that people who are well off are simply not interested in the tragedies of other people. Now I see that people actually are not interested in truth, goodness, justice, and meaning. I understand that the masters of the contemporary world—Western politicians—are catastrophically wrong in their belief that what does not directly threaten them does not concern them, that they can preserve their prosperity if they are lenient about an aggression that happens "somewhere far away."

I now understand that much of what made my life bearable is simply an illusion; I now understand that all my images of the West and the so-called free world were an illusion; I now understand that even here, in the West, they do not look at me as a person but as a member of a certain group. That is why, after all my experiences, after the loss of a great number of my illusions, it is much harder to endure life and the world today, and your letter is in a way responsible for that. My book, *Sarajevo, Exodus of a City*, which I wrote for you last year, is the first part of my response to your letter; this belated reply is the second part; I am afraid that the third part of my response will be some future book, bitter and utterly devoid of hope.

Yours,
Dzevad Karahasan
Salzburg, Austria
July 1994

A LOVE LETTER

To Dragana Tomasevic Karahasan
Sarajevo

My dear, beautiful, only one,
Here is another of those miracles that has followed us in the
past year. We are beginning to literally live my literature; our
lives are becoming, as literally as possible, parallel to the characters in the novels which we have first imagined, and then written
down together. Do you remember that beautiful time, about ten
years ago, when I started working on the first part of *Eastern
Divan?* How we discussed every sentence from Begzada's* letters, and how you used to say, as the ultimate argument, that you
knew far better how Begzada would write, not only because you
are a woman like her, but also because I conceived Begzada with
you in mind? Could we have anticipated, in those discussions,
what is happening to us now—that we are becoming like the
characters whom we have shaped in our own images? Do you
remember how you once said that you love Begzada, but that
you would not want to get to know her destiny through actual
experience—of loving your husband through letters? Playfully
reproaching me, you told me then that you know that I am ready
to do this, because my emotional stance toward writing and my
ethical radicalism—closer to the Middle Ages than to this
time—oblige me to be ready to live what I have written. I admit-
ted that you were right, and I tried to convince you that you fit
that time as well, regardless of how much at home you might
feel in this one. Have I not arrived in this era because of you?
The truth is that the fourteenth century is closer to me than this

---

* A character in *Eastern Divan.*

time; it is true that I would feel better among those people than among today's writers who think that life does not oblige them to write, and that what they write does not obligate them to anything special in their lives. But I was born today and you love me. I think that I was born today because of you, so that you would find your husband, and so that our love, which someone may have written down in that other era of mine, would be realized in this life. Because of that you belong to my time as much as I belong to this time of yours, and I thank you for that.

But, did it have to happen, my God, that we would really experience what we have imagined, sensed, and then wrote? It seems as if it had to happen, and that is good, I suppose. I talk to you in my thoughts, I feel you and love you, absent as you are, equally strongly as I did when we were in the same room; it is good for me to know that you exist somewhere, and that you are nonetheless present in me. More present than people I look at and whom I touch, more present than the clothes I wear, more present than hunger that I feel from time to time. It is good and beautiful that I know about you.

I am not even shy anymore, as you can see: I am writing to you through newspapers. That shy, sickly, introverted husband of yours who could not hold you by the hand in the presence of a third person. This war has the merit of having liberated me from shyness. The first letter I have sent you, through a journalist, Walter, was taken by the Serb soldiers at Ilidza,* together with Walter's car, camera, and the rest. I felt terrible when I found out about that. I thought I would not live through that night. My letter, full of love, caring, tenderness—being held and read by an unwashed vagabond, capable of raping, killing a child, shooting rockets at a city. Terrible. Sickening, humiliating, and cynical.

---

* A resort on the the outskirts of Sarajevo.

And then—when I felt I would have to kill myself if I survived that night, because one could not and should not live after such a person had read our letter—at one moment, literally in a flash of understanding (enlightenment?), it became clear to me that he could not really read that letter. He could see the letters, he could utter every word spelled in those letters, but he could not understand that which was written there, because it was written in the tongue of love, which is absolutely unintelligible to him, because he has never known something similar (remember how shabbily written the love episodes were in the novels of the ideologues of Serb fascism?).

We are protected from them! They may be able to hear the tongue of love that flows between us, as an acoustic phenomenon, but they cannot understand it, and because of that they cannot really apprehend it.

In the same way that it has built bridges in time, connecting my time with yours, our love has built a wall around us in space, behind which we are completely protected from them and from all that belongs to them. Because of that I am neither ashamed nor afraid anymore—I know that we are, thanks to our love, beyond all evil, and that we will talk to each other every night as we have done so far. I know that you hear what I am telling you, and I know that owing to that this life of mine is bearable. Thank you.

Your Dzevad

9 May, in the second year of the War
Klagenfurt, Austria *

---

* This letter was published in a Zagreb periodical less than three weeks before Dragana Tomasevic Karahasan joined her husband in Austria, ending their three-month separation.

Afterword

Dzevad Karahasan comes from a destroyed country.

I, too, come from the same country. Only three years ago it was our common country, called Yugoslavia. Now I live in Croatia and he lives in exile in Austria. And I am much better off, because at least I know the name of my country. Karahasan does not even know that. Is it Bosnia and Herzegovina? Or Bosnia? Or only Herzegovina? Or perhaps this country by now has its fourth and new name, if it is not already swallowed up by other countries surrounding it?

It was not so long ago when Dzevad Karahasan could travel by a direct train from Sarajevo to Zagreb. Imagine, it was as easy and took as little time as traveling from New York to Boston. I know it is hard to believe all that now, but believe it or not, such a train ride was a normal, common practice. In those days I met him in Zagreb. Tall and pale, he was dressed oddly in a black suit, as if he were about to attend a funeral. He smoked heavily, and I remember that his manner of speaking—slowly, with long pauses—struck me as somehow Middle Eastern. Back then, we spent several hours talking. I do not recall the exact topic of our conversations, or if it was even about something important or not. But such meetings became important at the moment when we could not see each other anymore, and I could not visit with anyone else from Sarajevo, for that matter. After April 1992, such a trip was an inconceivable excursion, a trip on the edge of suicide. Yugoslavia was torn apart like an old rug. The city of Sarajevo became a sort of concentration camp, which one could enter only with the greatest difficulty, and from which one could hardly get out. In besieged Sarajevo people lived and starved, lost hope, and got killed at random. Not systematically like in Auschwitz, where it happened according to precise lists and through a chimney. I don't think it is possible even to compare Sarajevo and Auschwitz, but there is at least one aspect where comparison seems possible: both Sarajevo under siege and Auschwitz represent a closed system, with their own sets of rules and patterns of human behavior. And every closed system where people get killed and one is uncertain about the future, produces a certain kind of psychology that is not easy to understand.

I sometimes have felt the same, because I too write about the war in the Balkans. While traveling around and talking about my experiences and my book *The Balkan Express*, I felt that misunderstanding followed me like a heavy suitcase or a stray dog. Perhaps "misunderstanding" is too strong a word; what I really mean is the different perspective of the outsider and the insider. It is not the same if you live in a country at war, such as Croatia, or in a country at peace, such as the United States. But even if Croatia and Bosnia both are experiencing a war, it still makes all the difference in the world if you live in Zagreb or Sarajevo. Zagreb was not shelled. From that point of view, Dzevad Karahasan is indeed an insider and perhaps from one of the last circles of Dante's "Inferno." I am only an apprentice.

I believed, however, that because we both are writers born in the same country, because we belong to the same generation and speak the same language, I could easily understand Karahasan's writing on the war. But it was not so. War is first of all chaos, but within that chaos there are degrees, extremes, nuances of what one sees and feels. We both experienced the war, but we write about it differently. Imagine it as two ends of a set of binoculars; if you look through it from one end, you will see faraway things appear close. If you look through it from the other end, you will see the very same objects appear farther away. How, then, are we to understand each other if our perspectives are so different?

Or better, how to read Dzevad Karahasan?

I remember exactly when I first took *Sarajevo, Exodus of a City* into my hands and started to read it. It was on a cold day last winter. At that time the radio reported that the temperature in Sarajevo dropped under minus 10 degrees Farenheit, that convoys were not coming through, that food was being rationed, and that people perhaps would have to face famine. I sat in my warm room. I felt guilty. Not because I was not in Sarajevo—thanks God that I was not—or because I had more than two slices of bread per day—thanks God I had. I felt guilty for a completely different reason: Because I am a writer and I have been writing on the war over the last three years; I did this because I believed that my words would make a difference.

That very morning, when I took Karahasan's book into my hands, an editor had asked me to write on Sarajevo again: "You know, the second winter for the besieged city, no food, the slow dying...." Yes, I know, I said, already depressed. And of course I knew. I had enough imagination to write about the feelings of a person who has to live there, with minus ten degrees, no heating, a little food, and barely any hope—I have met such people. But it had no sense any longer, it was impossible to continue to write about Sarajevo, or about the war itself. At least I felt that I could not do it any longer. I had to admit to myself that I had run out of words. All of a sudden, I became acutely aware that I had said all that I could. Not only did I realize that I had written about the surface, the first circle of that infernal war, but I felt my writing did not mean a thing. If words could change something, I thought, or save at least one life, the war would have been over long ago. More clearly than ever before, I felt my helplessness as a writer in front of something that people usually name *war*, but in fact is madness, chaos, and death. Perhaps a writer from Sarajevo could do it better, and then his writing, coming from the very center of hell, would have a different meaning?

Then I started to read Karahasan's book. His opening chapter, "Sarajevo, Portrait of an Internal City," is a sophisticated, poetic description of the city plan and its meaning. Under different circumstances I would perhaps love it, but in January this year, on that very cold day, the text seemed somehow wrong to me. How could it be, I asked myself, that Karahasan is writing about Sarajevo with such a distance, with such withheld emotions about his own city, turned into a symbol of suffering? His

approach disturbed me a lot, as if I myself—not Karahasan—
was in Sarajevo. As if my very house—and not his—had been
bombarded and my own relative had been killed...

Coincidentally or maybe not, at the same time I bought
another book, and started to read it along with *Sarajevo, Exodus
of a City*. It was Primo Levi's memoir, *Survival in Auschwitz*.
Finally, Karahasan's book became crystal clear to me. I was
able to see now that what I had interpreted as his "cold"—
that is, rational, controlled way of writing about the horrors
of the war, as if he was not really present there, as if snipers
were not threatening him every morning when he went out to
fetch food or water—came from his different experience of
the war itself. In other words, one insider helped me to
understand the other.

After reading Primo Levi, I could not interpret Karahasan
in the same way as before. I no longer read his book as an
attempt to escape reality and create distance between himself
and the world, but as an attempt to be present in the only way
he as a writer could be present—and to give that presence
some kind of meaning. Thus, the minute descriptions of
Sarajevo or his own part of the city, called Marindvor, are not
simple analysis, but *in memoriam* full of love for Sarajevo and
his home disappearing in front of his own eyes. By writing
about them, Karahasan is removing them into the only safe
place, that of his memory. Comparing Sarajevo to Jerusalem,
he says:

> Behind lowered eyelashes, I saw Sarajevo, so much ruined and
> so much loved—loved as never before—rising up from the
> earth, taking off and flying away, somewhere beyond, where

everything is gentle and tranquil. It flew toward the deepest recesses of reality, where it can be loved and dreamed about, to where it could shine back upon us, rich with meaning, like a beckoning destination.

In writing about Sarajevo, the act of writing itself was Karahasan's only possibility to re-conquer normal life and his home, if only in the text itself.

Upon his arrival at Auschwitz, Primo Levi describes a scene where he is surrounded by a mass of naked people and the absurdity of it all. He describes it as if "all of that was happening to someone else, and yet, it happened to me." Just because it is such a horrible experience, he has to go on trying to convince himself that it is reality, that this is happening to him, too. As life in the concentration camp gets worse, he mentally and emotionally feels more estranged from the reality of the camp. "I think of myself only a couple of minutes daily, and even then from a distance, like from the outside," he writes. That same kind of detached reaction I found in the Karahasan text:

> I kept staring at my own hands, as if checking their reality. One crushing effect of this war on those who actually fare the best—who have not been wounded or killed, that is—is this loss of confidence in reality, or at least in one's own ability to experience reality. They are losing their world in the same way I was losing my own house as I looked at it, discovering how beautiful it was.

He has to establish a distance from everyday terror, not a physical one, because that would be impossible under the circumstances—but at least a psychological distance. But such a distance may also be created in everyday behavior, by sticking to our normal rules and habits. Therefore, Karahasan insists that human beings should remain "cultural beings," that they should continue to use fork and knife, to say good day and good-bye, to write, paint or act, as if nothing is going on. His belief is that in this way people can defend their human dignity, as well as civilization itself.

Karahasan writes about his feelings in a restrained way, almost casually, listing facts and involving emotions in a very gentle way. One has to discover that not only was his own apartment hit by a shell or that his wife is Serbian, but also that his mother-in-law was killed because she had given shelter to two Muslim families. As if this destruction of his personal life represents only a small footnote to the war, to Bosnia falling apart. But there is something else to it. One could sense that he is using words in this particular way because they are not strong enough to convey reality. He, too, as Primo Levi indicated, seems to be in need of a new language to express these unbearable experiences. It may appear as a paradox that it perhaps was more difficult for Karahasan than for Primo Levi to express that reality. Dzevad Karahasan was in no way prepared for it. The experience of our postwar generation was not war, but forgetting that it had happened, not hatred, but tolerance, not conflict, but coexistence. Therefore, I believe that Karahasan instinctively economizes with his language. The condensed portrait of Sarajevo, his idealization of this city as a Paradise Lost, is a subdued lamentation, but still a lamentation, like the prophet Jeremiah's lamentation for his vanquished Jerusalem.

As I understand from this book, to write under these circumstances means trying to be stubbornly rational in a situation that makes it almost impossible to be so. In order to prevent the world around him from falling apart, he is controlling his emotions and his words very carefully. The most moving moment in Primo Levi's book is not a description of death—death is barely mentioned there—but an attempt to recall Dante's verses in order to prove to himself that he still is a human being. In Karahasan's book, it is perhaps not the descriptions of fear that touch us the most, but the story of a misunderstanding between him and his French visitor. In a way, this is the central theme of his documentary prose on the war. It is not his personal emotional drama and the changes he is forced to go through, but the drama of the destruction of a multi-ethnic and culturally pluralist society. Karahasan is convinced that this is the cause of the war; as nation-states are formed in the Balkans from the parts of the former Yugoslavia, this sort of diversity cannot be accepted— therefore it must be destroyed. His French visitor, even if well intentioned, does not understand the difference between their two cultures:

> We tried, we tried really hard. Yet we never understood each other. We could not help it; the differences between our two cultures would not permit it. My culture—inherently polyphonous, pluralistic, and dialogical; and his—inherently unitary, monological, and homogeneous.

In almost every story, Karahasan comes back to the loss of tolerance between nations, cultures, and religions, and this hurts him more than his personal problems, the cold, or the lack of water. His insistence on the importance of values, like cultural pluralism, cosmopolitanism, tolerance, and morality, at the time when his own life is in jeopardy, is indeed an attempt of the very same kind as that of trying to remember Dante's verses.

However, even if the writer himself is a victim, *Sarajevo, Exodus of a City* does not read like a book we would expect from a victim; that is, an outcry of pain. With this book of documentary prose on the war, Dzevad Karahasan is a witness of a very special kind. When I say this, I mean that we all share a common belief in the importance of historical documents simply because we all believe that we can learn something from them. We learn in order to change, to improve as human beings, to not repeat mistakes. Humanity is reformable, we believe. Yet, this is exactly my problem: I do not share this belief any longer. Because of this Balkan war, I do not believe that our recorded experience can improve or change us very much.

In 1946, when he wrote his book after having been liberated from Auschwitz, Primo Levi wanted his experience to serve us as a warning. He repeated this wish in the postscript he wrote in 1976: We should remember the horrors of war and genocide in order not to repeat them. But nearly fifty years later, in the middle of Europe, we are witnessing the very same drama again—war and an attempted genocide. It is happening in a generation that was brought up on the stories about the Holocaust, because its parents had seen it and many had even suffered in it themselves. The question, then, is simple: What is the use of this writing, of documenting horrors? I am afraid that the simple answer *"To warn"* is no longer valid. I don't believe that documentary prose can be expected to work in that way any longer.

Therefore, when I finished reading Karahasan's book, I was still bothered by something I think is relevant for both Karahasan and me. Why do we write? Does it make any sense to document the war at all, when it is bound to happen again? My own experience with this war tells me that to write is, above all, to try to establish some kind of order in chaos. In a general sense, writing itself is the proof that human beings can behave rationally, and this might be its only purpose. As it is possible to kill, it is also possible to write. Didn't George Orwell, in one of his essays, write, "While I write, highly civilized human beings are flying over my head trying to kill me"? On the one hand, a house destroyed during war is as much evidence of what human beings are capable of as any text on the same war. But I think we should give up the illusion that we learn from any of these experiences. We don't. On the other hand, if war is the negation of humanity, documentary prose is its affirmation. More than that, I am afraid we should not hope for, either as writers or as human beings.

Dzevad Karahasan is out of Sarajevo, in some "safe" place in Austria. He is now a refugee. I recently read an interview with him. How do you feel in this situation? a journalist asked him. Karahasan does not give the straightforward answer a reader might expect; he does not say he is happy because he survived, or that he is out of danger. He only says that he lives well and that his books are published. But he lives in despair, at the verge of suicide. "The language I think in, I feel in, I live in and experience the world in, is reduced to an instrument for producing misunderstandings," he says. Out of Sarajevo, he now has to fight in order to survive as a writer, being deprived of the landscape of his language.

When I think of him, when I see him in my mind, tall and perhaps still dressed in black, I remember again Primo Levi. I pray that Karahasan does not have the same horrifying, repetitive dream that haunted Levi in Auschwitz. In the dream, he is finally at home. All his family is gathered around the table, they are eating together and Primo Levi is telling them the terrible story of his imprisonment in the concentration camp. But no one listens. They are indifferent, chatting about other things as if he is not there.

As if nothing ever happened...

July 1994
Vienna

ABOUT THE AUTHOR

Dzevad Karahasan was born in Tomislavgrad, a town in southwest Bosnia, in 1953. He moved to Sarajevo in 1972. He was graduated with a degree in literature and drama from the University of Sarajevo in 1976, and received his doctorate in drama from the University of Zagreb in 1986. Since then he has been affiliated with the Academy of Theatrical Arts at the University of Sarajevo, first as a lecturer, then as an associate professor. He has been artistic director of several Yugoslavian national theater festivals. In 1992, after the war in Bosnia-Herzegovina and the siege of Sarajevo had begun, he was elected dean of the Academy. In February 1993 Karahasan fled Sarajevo, determined to publish this book, his eleventh, in the West. It has also been published in Croatian, German, Dutch, Italian, and French editions. His other works range from drama to criticism to fiction. He and his wife, Dragana Tomasević, are now living in Salzburg, Austria.

KODANSHA GLOBE

International in scope, this series offers distinguished books that explore the lives, customs, and mindsets of peoples and cultures around the world.

MAN MEETS DOG
Konrad Lorenz
Illustrated by Konrad Lorenz
    and Annie Eisenmenger
New introduction by
    Donald McCaig
Translated by
    Marjorie Kerr Wilson
1-56836-051-7
$12.00

**SARAJEVO, EXODUS OF
A CITY**
Dzevad Karahasan
Afterword by
    Slavenka Drakulić
Translated by
    Slobodan Drakulić
1-56836-057-6
$10.00

MERCHANT PRINCES
*An Intimate History
    of Jewish Families
    Who Built Great
    Department Stores*
Leon Harris
New introduction by
    Kenneth Libo
New foreword by
    Oscar Handlin
1-56836-044-4
$15.00

**THE FORBIDDEN
    EXPERIMENT**
*The Story of the Wild
    Boy of Aveyron*
Roger Shattuck
New introduction by
    Douglas Keith Candland
1-56836-048-7
$13.00

TURKESTAN REUNION
Eleanor Holgate
    Lattimore
Illustrations by Eleanor
    Frances Lattimore
1-56836-053-3
$13.00

HIGH TARTARY
Owen Lattimore
Original photographs by
    Owen Lattimore
New introduction by
    Orville Schell
1-56836-054-1
$15.00

GOD'S LAUGHTER
*Physics, Religion, and
    the Cosmos*
Gerhard Staguhn
1-56836-045-2
$13.00

**THE FOUR-CORNERED
    FALCON**
*Essays on the Interior
    West and the Natural
    Scene*
Reg Saner
1-56836-049-5
$14.00

THE CROSSING PLACE
*A Journey Among the
    Armenians*
Philip Marsden
New introduction by
    Peter Sourian
1-56836-052-5
$13.00

TRACING IT HOME
A Chinese Journey
Lynn Pan
1-56836-043-6
$12.00

**TRESPASSERS ON THE
    ROOF OF THE WORLD**
*The Secret Exploration
    of Tibet*
Peter Hopkirk
1-56836-050-9
$13.00

To order, contact your local bookseller or call 1-800-788-6262 (mention code G1). For a complete listing of titles, please contact the Kodansha Editorial Department at Kodansha America, Inc., 114 Fifth Avenue, New York, NY 10011.